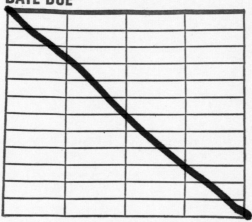

LEGITIMACY AND STABILITY IN LATIN AMERICA

LEGITIMACY AND STABILITY IN LATIN AMERICA

A Study of Chilean Political Culture

by Francisco José Moreno

New York   New York University Press
London   University of London Press Limited

1969

*To Susan, Joëlle, and Jessica — and also
to Sombra and Humo*

Acknowledgments

To acknowledge intellectual debts is an impossible task. After years of thinking, reading, and talking about certain problems it is no longer possible to remember what ideas came from where. I would like to think that all the conceptions presented in this book are the products of my own mind, but I must accept the improbability of such an assumption. Since I do not remember exactly what I owe to whom I will just list, as best I can, those who in one way or another have influenced the development of the ideas expressed in this book.

With Jorge Tallet I have discussed Latin American politics for the last seventeen years. Many of my ideas have been clarified by his perceptive mind. Francisco O. Baeza and Fermín Flores were of great assistance in helping me to give intellectual life to my political militancy. José Antonio Echeverría, José Iglesias, and Pepe el Cínico provided first-hand examples of charismatic leadership.

In Chile I owe special thanks to Mario Góngora, Jaime Eyzaguirre, and Hernán Godoy. I am also most grateful to Stanley Rothman who was kind enough to take me along to interviews with Eduardo Frei and Raúl Ampuero.

Ted Gurr read the manuscript and I am sure that where I have not followed his suggestions the book has lost in perceptiveness and clarity. Maria Christina Franke has typed the manuscript more times than she or I care to remember. Her assistance has been manyfold. She has been a helpful critic and her suggestions have saved me from costly errors.

The Pan American Union and the New York University Graduate School of Arts and Science supplied the funds for my stay in Chile and subsequent research.

Contents

Introduction

All books on politics are partisan. Sometimes the author's political convictions are clearly stated; other times they are submerged under layers of academic rhetoric. Any careful look at scholarly analyses of political problems would show, sooner or later, commitments to specific values and beliefs.

There is nothing objectionable about having political opinions and points of view. As a matter of fact, in a cultural-ideological sense, they are unavoidable. Authors who try to hide their personal opinions while inadvertently attempting to guide the reader in a predetermined direction could be criticized on ethical grounds. More practical objections could also be raised against those who are unaware that, under their academic claims to objectivity and impartiality, they are promoting specific moral and political conceptions. The second group is, in some ways, more dangerous than the first. These authors have usually assimilated the values of their own culture to such a degree that they cannot recognize the relative and ethnocentric character of their beliefs. When they are analyzing foreign ideas and institutions, they usually transform their culture-bound political conceptions into absolute truths and view political phenomena only in reference to degrees of conformity to their own ideal patterns.

There are differences in degree, but all political studies are affected by the observer's cultural and psychological perspective. To conceal one's own political commitments only misleads or confuses the reader. Scientifically, the value of an author's contribution will be judged not on how uncommitted he is, but in how acutely he describes and interprets the subject under study. Therefore, I feel justified in taking a few lines to explain the political perspective from which this book has been written.

In the pages that follow I relate the potential for political stability in Latin America to cultural forces active in the area. I try to show, using Chile as a case study, that it is through acceptance, rather than rejection, of those cultural elements, that political stability can be attained in the countries of the area. At no point do I intend to justify morally, or suggest a preference for, traditional values and institutions. Neither do I see in stability per se a desirable goal. I acknowledge, though, that the continuity of institutional arrangements can only exist to the degree they incorporate into themselves given cultural tendencies. And I do believe there is something to be gained by accepting reality. My personal preference would be to establish societies in which the possibilities for change, experimentation, and improvement would be limitless. Unfortunately, it is unlikely that this type of society will evolve. The second best alternative would be to establish societies in which any potential forces for a better life that might exist can be used to the greatest extent possible. The first step in this direction is to know what those potentials are.

In bringing forth the Latin American and Chilean tendencies toward monistic and idealistic rule my intention is to discover how meaningful change can be brought about. I assume that cultural forces do not have to play an immutable social and economic role. The tendency toward charismatic leadership, for example, does not only produce a Diego Potales; it can also bring about a Rómulo Betancourt or a Fidel Castro.

Latin Americans have been, at least since independence, under great internal and external pressure to adopt institutional devices alien to their cultural and historical traditions. This exercise in daydreaming and wishful thinking has tended to preclude, rather than to accelerate, the implementation of changes affecting the social, economic, and political well-being of the region's inhabitants. Such forces have also undermined political creativity and originality. The main theme of this book is to show the futility of this imitative process.[1] My basic contention is that whatever objectives Latin American communities may be pursuing at the moment, their best chance to attain them is through the use and development of their own cultural and political tools, rather than through the borrowing of alien prescriptions.

The process of imitating foreign models is of doubtful convenience for the direct attainment of desired goals, and it has a negative psychological by-product as well. It increases dependence on outsiders and allows Latin

---

1. In the Latin American tendency to imitate some magic elements seem to exist. Sigmund Freud has dealt at some length with the magic connotation of the imitative process in primitive societies. His conclusions, it seems to me, are equally applicable to contemporary societies. See his "Animism, Magic and the Omnipotence of Thoughts" in *Totem and Taboo: Some Points of Agreement between the Mental Lives of Savages and Neurotics* (New York: W. W. Norton & Company, Inc. 1950), pp. 75ff.

Americans to evade responsibility for their own short-comings.

The adoption of certain institutional devices has sometimes been confused, by analysts of Latin America, with actual change in the character of the functions performed. Copying foreign models has been accepted as a sign of substantial change. What Osvaldo Sunkel has said about Chilean economic development could be said of all Latin American politics. "They have shown great flexibility in absorbing elements of modernization, without the need to alter their basic structure."[2] The concept that a basic alteration in the political traditions of Latin America is necessary in order to change the substance of governmental policies and decisions is questionable. Such an assumption leads directly to over-concern for the form and tends to disregard the substance of political activities. The question is not, for example, whether persons or interests are represented by an effective legislature, or through an all-powerful executive. The question is how many are represented and how effectively.

The social and economic plight of most Latin Americans is not going to be ended by any restructure of the formal political apparatus. It will be ended, if it is ever going to happen, by a direct attack on the substantive problems themselves. When the time for the attack comes, the native institutions will prove the only reliable ones. Their strength will not be based on any abstraction that history and culture may exercise, but on the psychological reality they represent. Institutions are, after all, mechanisms of social dynamics that must be operated by members

2. "Change and Frustration in Chile" in Claudio Veliz (ed.), *Obstacles to Change in Latin America* (New York: Oxford University Press, 1969), p. 117.

of a given community. To the degree the individuals involved accept and understand these mechanisms they will operate successfully. To the degree the mechanisms are alien to the experience and psychological orientations of those involved they will fail. In time of crisis, or of profound change, the need to operate with known and acceptable institutions would probably tend to increase rather than decrease.

Aside from the general objectives already described, this book has more specific goals. It attempts to contribute to the understanding of the relationship between legitimacy and stability in Chile, and it challenges, sometimes explicitly and sometimes implicitly, some generalized historical and political assumptions. In the process it tries to identify some of the most salient characteristics of Chilean political culture.

The relationship between legitimacy and stability is basic to the life of any political system. If we understand legitimacy not as a legal concept, but as the psychological acceptance by the members of a given community of a series of institutional and relationship arrangements that would determine and control their political life, we would be dealing with one of the most crucial aspects of politics. As Harry Eckstein tells us, "a government will tend to be stable if its authority pattern is congruent with the other authority patterns of the society of which it is a part."[3]

---

3. *Division and Cohesion in Democracy: A Study of Norway* (Princeton: Princeton University Press, 1966), p. 234. José Martí put forward the same idea in a more poetic form when he said: "With a decree of Hamilton you cannot stop the horse of a Venezuelan cowboy. With a phrase of Sieyès you cannot make the coagulated blood of the Indian race circulate. . . . the spirit or the government must spring from the nation." "Nuestra América" in *Obras Completas* (Havana: Editorial Lex, 1948), Vol. II, p. 107.

This basically means that there must be a close and direct relationship between the political organization and the traditions, mores, and value system of a given community. A government tends to be unstable to the degree it tends to depart from the traditional values and institutional understanding of the community. On the other hand, to the degree the government conforms to the traditions of the community, it would tend to be stable. Therefore, in order to evaluate the chances for survival of any political arrangement we must look beyond the institutional arrangement itself, to the community in question—its traditional form of organization, the way in which conflicts and problems are solved, and whatever other characteristics of social behavior we may be able to detect. Only after we have obtained a general idea as to what patterns of political organization and behavior are acceptable to the community, will we be in a position to make intelligent estimates about the operational success of the political system under analysis.

In prodding into the political culture of Chile and Latin America, and in developing the theory put forward in this book, I have relied not only on the written material refered to in the footnotes and quotes, but also on my own experience as a Latin American. Although I would be the first one to acknowledge important differences between any of the countries in the Ibero-American world, I firmly believe that we are very much talking about a single political culture. Therefore, I have relied heavily on my own experience and non-intellectual instruments of perception. Without going to the extreme of denying outsiders the ability to derive proper conclusions as to the patterns of behavior of a given group of people, I would emphasize the need to be aware of subtle, emotional currents which are usually only perceivable to the members of the group. By and large, I believe that the literature in English concerning Latin American politics ignores some of the most fundamental psychological mechanisms that operate in those societies. In all fairness, not only outsiders have been guilty of this omission, but in a different way, and for different reasons, insiders have also frequently tended to ignore some of the most basic psychological characteristics of Latin American political behavior.[4]

It would be presumptuous of me to claim that this book does anything beyond raising a few issues for further discussion. The relationship between legitimacy and stability, as well as the character and nature of legitimacy itself, must be broken down into their cultural and psychological components. The understanding of external as well as the internal machinery through which political institutions and political leaderships are accepted or rejected is one of our most pressing problems. It is in fact through the study of legitimacy that we can build a useful bridge between the study of individual and social psychology, and the analysis of political behavior. As a child and as a young adult in Cuba, I can clearly remember how patterns of leadership selection and modes of social organization were quite different from what they seem to be in a country like the United States. I say what they seem to be, because after more than twelve years of residing in this country I am still not sure that I emotionally understand some of the dynamics of social behavior prevalent in America. For example, I can see intellectually how there appears to be a certain compulsive mechanism that forces members of the American social and cultural community to accept the rule of the majority.

---

4. F. J. Moreno, "Latin America: The Fear Within" in *The Yale Review*, Vol. LV, No. 2 (December 1965), pp. 161ff.

I have observed such behavior in small groups, at faculty meetings, at meetings of parents associations, and in a variety of similar instances. I do not understand, since I have never experienced it, what mechanism compels any member of any of those groups to accept the will of other people just because they constitute a group larger than the one to which he belongs. When I grew up my community, and the educational system in turn, taught me that whenever the majority was in disagreement with me, the majority was wrong, and the only intelligent and acceptable action was to disregard the will of the majority and to stick to what I thought was correct. On the other hand, I was taught a greater degree of submission to the family than the one I seem to detect among Americans.

My own experience seems to indicate that there are probable distinctions in the ways that Latin Americans and Americans perceive their participation in group activities. If these distinctions reflect different forms of social behavior, or if they symbolize dissimilar dynamic forces at work, they must be deeply consequential to the political structures these communities are able to develop. In my analysis of Chile I have relied heavily on my own experience for the evaluation of the roles of certain cultural forces. I have put aside any pretensions of being a Latin Americanist and I have looked at Chile simply as a Latin American.

The Child's Toys & the Old Man's Reasons
Are the Fruits of the Two Seasons.
The Questioner, who sits so sly,
Shall never know how to Reply.

William Blake

LEGITIMACY AND STABILITY
IN LATIN AMERICA

1.

*T*he *C*olonial *H*eritage

The past does not necessarily hold the key to the present, but it can certainly contribute to its understanding. An analysis of traditional Spanish legal thought and institutions will throw light on the nature and structure of the colonial organization as well as upon the psychological and social orientations underlying the role of law. Legal systems are important not only because they provide explicit directives for the organization of the community, but also because when compared with the reality they are supposed to regulate, their study implies an evaluation of some of the most intricate mechanisms of the societies in question.

A substantive analysis of the colonial legal organization cannot be limited to a recapitulation of laws and regulations. Such an approach, although of a certain historical and institutional value, would disregard the social and political realities of the colonies. Literature on the subject has so far failed to delve into the most fundamental characteristics of Spanish legal behavior. Analysts have generally been concerned with evaluating, from predetermined moral positions, the contents of the legal prescriptions rather than investigating the nature of the lawmaking process. Thus, lengthy disquisitions on the moral and philosophical qualities of the Spanish legal dispositions have been made which, although often beautifully written, tend to be of little help in understanding the legal and political systems created by Spain.

Interpretations of the colonial past that have placed heavy emphasis on the evaluation of legal clauses and their provisions offer inadequate clues about the actual social and political conditions prevailing is those days.[1] Colonial Hispanic America had long texts providing for a detailed organization of power and for an almost perfect chain of command going from "His Royal and Caesarean Majesty" to the most remote *cabildo*.[2] But Spanish laws only seldom crystallized into political action and only rarely did the content of their provisions mold colonial political behavior.[3]

The failure of the law to reflect actual circumstances is not unique to Spain or to Spanish colonial legislation. Differences between law and reality exist in every society. What becomes worthwhile, then, is to determine the extent of these differences and to evaluate their social and political implications. In the case of Spain, a clear idea of the character and ramifications of this phenomenon is vital. The political legacy of Spain and its influence on

1. Bailey W. Diffie, *Latin American Civilization* (Harrisburg, Pennsylvania: Stackpole and Sons, 1945), p. 270; and Russell H. Fitzgibbon and Flaud C. Wooton, *Latin American Past and Present* (Boston: D.C. Heath and Co., 1946), p. 144.

2. The detailed organization of the colonies is clearly stated in the compilation of colonial laws ordered by the king of Spain in 1681. The official title of this collection of laws is *Recopilación de las leyes de los reynos de las Indias*.

3. Lucas Ayarragaray, *La anarquía argentina y el caudillismo* (Buenos Aires: Felix la Jouane y Cía., Editores, 1904), p. 34.

the colonies can only be comprehended if the relationship between the Spanish concept of law and reality is understood.

The Spanish Concept of Law

The Spanish ideas concerning law have a definite Roman origin.[4] From 219 B.C. to 409 A.D. the Iberian peninsula was under the control of the Roman legions and under the domination of Roman culture. During those centuries Roman institutions and thought became deeply rooted in the people of Iberia.[5] The language of the Romans became, in modified versions, the language of the peninsula. And with the Latin language, Roman legal thinking became a part of the Iberian way of life. Roman ideas and power did not, however, develop uniformly throughout Spain; the influence of Roman judicial principles was felt more in some areas than in others. Catalonia and the Basque country showed for many centuries a lesser degree of "romanization" than Castile. But in spite of such regional distinctions, Roman institutions and ideas gained a permanent and expanding grip over the people of the region.[6]

4. For a discussion of the influence of Roman law upon Spanish legal institutions and political thought see Marie R. Madden, *Political Theory and Law in Medieval Spain* (New York: Fordham University Press, 1930), pp. 1ff. For a detailed analysis of the development of some of the Spanish medieval legal institutions where Roman influence is easily detectable see Paulo Merêa, *Estudos de dereito hispânico medieval* (Coimbra, 1952).

5. Constantino Lascaris Comneno in his introduction to Marcelino Menéndez y Pelayo, *La filosofía española* (Madrid: Ediciones Rialp, S.A. 1955), traces the origin of Spanish philosophy to Seneca.

6. For example, two ancient Catalonian codes, *Las costumbres* of Tortosa and the *Usatges* of Barcelona, reflect definite Roman tendencies.

The acceptance of Roman law and of its implicit philosophical bases determined the direction of Spanish political thought and institutional development. The idealism and universalism which had found judicial and political expression in the *Ius Honorarium, Ius Naturale,* and *Ius Gentium* became an integral part of the Spanish way of thinking. The ethical connotations implied in the term *Ius*[7] began to undermine the legal validity of peninsular customs and traditions.[8] The writings of St. Isidore of Seville (*circa* 560–636) appear to have been heavily influenced by Roman concepts, although it must be remembered that when he wrote, the earthly idealism of Cicero had yielded to the spiritual ethics of Christianity.[9] The ideas of St. Isidore found institutional expression in the *Lex Visighotorum,* or *Fuero Juzgo,* the first Spanish compilation of laws of which we have recorded evidence.[10]

Roman ideas and institutions were not the only external factors shaping Spanish thought and behavior. For centuries, both Arabic and Germanic influences were

---

7. On the theory of *Ius* see R. W. Carlyle and A. J. Carlyle, *A History of Medieval Political Theory in the West* (Edinburgh: William Blackwood and Sons, 1903), Vol. II, pp. 13ff. See also John Bowle, *Western Political Thought from the Origins to Rousseau* (London: University Paperbacks, 1961. First published in 1947), pp. 82f.
8. Ewart Lewis, *Medieval Political Ideas* (London: Routledge and Kegan Paul, 1954), Vol. I, p. 5.
9. For a discussion of the Roman influence on the works of St. Isidore see Madden, *op. cit.,* pp. 19ff.; and Carlyle and Carlyle, *op. cit.,* Vol. I, pp. 221f.
10. This group of laws is also known under the following names: *Codex Legum, Liber gothorum, Liber judicum,* and *Forum judicum.* This last name gave origin during the thirteenth century to the Spanish title *Fuero de los jueces* of which *Fuero Juzgo* is a contraction. See Tomas W. Palmer Jr., *Guide to the Law and Legal Literature of Spain* (Washington, D.C.: Government Printing Office, 1915), pp. 26ff.

also to be found in the peninsula. The Germanic institutions of private law seem to have remained very much in use until at least the thirteenth century.[11] The Arabic contribution to Spanish political and legal life is somewhat more difficult to estimate. Institutionally, the extent of this influence could be and has been debated interminably. The fact that most of the Moslem invaders were not Arabs but Moors who marched into the country in different waves and at different stages of cultural development complicates the picture even more. These circumstances, combined with the later expulsion from Spain of great numbers of the followers of Islam, seem to indicate that the Islamic influence can be more easily detected in general cultural traits than in specific legal or political institutions.[12]

Notwithstanding the influence of other factors, the principles of Roman thought found fertile ground in the peninsula. The success of Latin ideas and institutions was intimately connected with the dominant position held by Castile among the several Spanish kingdoms. Of all the regional monarchies, Castile was the most powerful and

---

11. This is the generally accepted interpretation. See Eduardo de Hinojosa, *El elemento germánico en el derecho español* (Madrid: Imprenta Clásica Española, 1915). Lascaris, *op.cit.*, disagrees with this interpretation. He expresses doubt as to the Germanic origin of the Goths, and then goes on to assert that even if they were of German origin, by the time they reached the Iberian peninsula their institutions had been greatly influenced by those of Rome. This same author attaches to the Franks, who came to Spain much later, all responsibility for the establishment of Germanic legal institutions.

12. For general appraisals of the Islamic influence in Spain see Claudio Sánchez-Albornoz, *La España musulmana: según los autores islamitas y cristianos medievales* (Second Edition; Buenos Aires: Editorial "El Ateneo," 1960); and E. Lévi-Provençal, *La civilisation arabe en Espagne* (Paris: G. P. Maisonneuve et Laróse, 1961).

the least traditional. Founded *circa* 950, it was one of the last Iberian monarchies to emerge, but soon after its birth it was in control of the peninsula's central areas, leading the fight against the Moors. These two factors— its relatively recent birth and its leadership in the struggle against the infidel—placed Castile in a propitious position to utilize the universalist and ethical principles embodied in the laws of Rome.

Reality versus Law

In Rome, especially during the later part of the republic and the empire, law was neither a systematization of communal customs nor an attempted embodiment in legal precepts of the local traditions. Law was for the Romans, above everything else, a moral interpretation of life—an effort to define those ethical goals that the political community should strive to attain. The works of Cicero, Seneca, and the later Roman lawyers suggest examples of this interpretation of the legal function.[13] Law became an attempt, based upon abstract ethical reasoning, to determine how people ought to behave. This concept of law stimulated a search for theoretical perfection that soon became unconcerned with the ways in which people actually behaved. The trend away from custom and tradition can be easily discerned in the ascendancy that *Ius Honorarium, Ius Naturale,* and *Ius Gentium* gained upon *Ius Civile.*

The predominance of the ethical principle over ancestral custom was reflected in the famous Latin expression: *Est quidem vera lex, recta ratio congruens.* Reason,

---

13. For comments on the character of Roman law see Carlyle and Carlyle, *op. cit.,* Vol. I., pp. 1ff.; and George H. Sabine, *A History of Political Theory* (New York: Holt, Rinehart and Winston, Inc., 1961), pp. 158ff.

as the ability to discern between right and wrong according to predetermined abstract moral principles, was established as the main source of law. Reason, in the way used by the Roman jurists and philosophers, should not be confused with the ability to learn from experience. Although it could be argued, as Hume did, that all ideas are reflections of our impressions of reality,[14] there would still be a marked difference between legislation that is founded on the observation and acceptance of actual circumstances, and legislation based upon the conclusions of a more abstract logical process.

The Roman attempt to legislate on the basis of reason was an expression of idealistic thinking. This emphasis on idealism becomes quite interesting when it is remembered that it reached its zenith in a Rome under the control of praetorian guards and imperial armies. Idealism and universalism seem to have imbued the law with an essentially unrealistic character. Roman legislation came to be identified with beautiful principles of conduct that were regularly honored in the breach.[15]

While the Stoic philosophy was dominant, the Romans derived their legal ideals from Nature and Reason. After the establishment of Christianity, the Church laid down the moral principles that were to govern the conduct of man. The original ethical tenets provided by the philosophers and lawyers were related to this world, but the doctrines forwarded by the Fathers of the Church

---

14. David Hume, *An Enquiry Concerning Human Understanding.* First published in 1758.
15. Vicente Arangio Ruíz, *Historia del derecho ramano* (Madrid: Instituto Editorial Reus, 1943,) pp. 268ff, calls attention to the dual character of Roman political life. See also Charles P. Sherman, *Roman Law in the Modern World* (New York: Baker, Voorhes and Co., 1937), Vol. I, pp. 50ff.

were primarily concerned with the next.[16] The legal framework was cleansed of pagan philosophical commitments and filled with Christian theology. Although the objectives of the law had been shifted to the realm of the spiritual, the basic nature of the system remained unchanged since its fundamental function was still to provide moral canons of conduct that society was meant to follow.[17] Whereas the final goal was moved from earthly perfection to the salvation of the soul, the basic structure of idealistic thinking did not suffer any major alteration.

In Spain, the *Etymologies* of St. Isidore and the provisions of the *Fuero Juzgo* were Christian in form and Roman in substance. From its very origins, written Spanish law was far more an expression of ideals to be attained than a reflection of social customs and traditions. The idealism and universalism of the Romans translated into Christian terminology gave form to the Spanish conception of law and politics. Customs and traditions then gave way to high-sounding ethical and spiritual principles as the source of law. The strength of ancient local habits was undermined by a legal system that claimed moral superiority. Law in the name of

16. Carlyle and Carlyle, *op. cit.,* Vol. I, pp. 81ff.; and Alfred Verdross, *Abendländische Rechtsphilosophie. Ihre Grundlagen und Hauptprobleme in geschichtlicher Schau* (Vienna, 1958), Section Two.

17. Adolf Waas, *Herrschaft und Staat im Frühmittelalter,* sees this idealistic inclination as characteristic of Christian thinking when he says "in the Germanic conception that which is law must continue to be so; in the Christian conception that which is law must become so." Carlyle and Carlyle *op. cit.,* Vol. III, p. 11, believe that the basic difference between Roman and Teutonic law is founded in the Roman concern with origins and the Teutonic concern with existing conditions. On the supremacy of the concept of Natural Law during the Middle Ages see Otto Gierke, *Political Theories of the Middle Ages* (Boston: Beacon Press, 1959. First published in 1900), pp. 73ff.

justice parted with reality. The fate of Spain was cast. Don Quixote, paying little heed to Sancho's counsel, began to charge the windmills.[18]

To appreciate the implications of such a conception of law, it is necessary to examine some aspects of idealistic and universalist thinking. An ideal conception is, when reduced to its psychological components, a rejection of reality; its implementation is always an attempt to replace an existing reality with an intellectual abstraction. Guido de Ruggiero defines idealism as "a tendency to oppose the representations of the mind to empirical reality and to give them a predominant position and role in the scale of human values."[19]

Idealism is a form of escapism—a way of avoiding or bypassing a distasteful reality. Judicial idealism is, among other things, an attempt to legislate problems out of existence. By undertaking to change reality through the enactment of legal regulations, judicial idealism vests upon the legal system a quasi-magical connotation. The idea that a wish, when expressed through the formalistic ritual of the law, should be able to alter reality appeals to psychological and anthropological tendencies probably present in all societies.

Universalism, as a theoretical concern for the whole in implicit disregard of the specific qualities of the parts, is but an expression of idealism. As such it was present in Roman legal thought and institutions. Idealistic and universalist concepts—which in the case of Rome could be legitimately traced to Platonic thought—are deductive-

---

18. For a most interesting analysis of the Spanish attitude toward law see Angel Ganivet, *Idearium español y el porvenir de España* (Madrid: Espasa-Calpe, S. A., 1962), pp. 53ff.
19. "Idealism" in Edwin R. A. Seligman and Alvin Johnson (editors), *Encyclopedia of the Social Sciences* (New York: The Macmillan Co., 1937), Vol. VII, p. 568.

ly derived and tend to be absolute in character and dogmatic in nature. Their predominance over the legal system indicates the acceptance of nonpragmatic principles of social and political organization.

As philosophical tendencies idealism and pragmatism are not necessarily exclusive of one another. Furthermore, it could be argued, that idealism as defined here cannot really exist in a perfect form. Idealism, if it is to have any impact on legal or political behavior, must be more than just an exercise in unrealistic reasoning. This trend of thought would lead to the conclusion that idealistic thinking is not only an abstract speculation, but also a tool to perform some very practical functions.[20]

Idealism presents at least two different aspects. In one, the content of the ideal formulas represents a denial of reality, and the use made of the formulas may be indicative of realistic awareness. While efforts to apply the ideal prescriptions would, by definition, be doomed to failure, the existence of the ideal formulation may be successfully performing a given social function. The other dimension to idealism exists apart from unrealistic thinking.

That the Spanish judicial system could be organized along Roman lines suggests the existence of similarities between both societies. Although it is a moot question whether the adoption of such a legal system required the presence of idealistic attitudes, or whether such attitudes resulted from the adoption of the system, there would seem to be little doubt that at least a certain basic inclination toward unrealistic, or escapist, thinking existed in

20. See Gaetano Mosca's theory of the political formula in *The Ruling Class,* a modified translation of his *Elementi di Scienza Politica,* (New York: McGraw-Hill Book Co., Inc., 1939), pp. 70f.

Spain before the system went into effect.[21] Once the system was adopted, the predispositions were ratified, assured, and enhanced. In the interminable process of action and counteraction, they in turn made the new institutions intelligible and acceptable to the people of the country.

The concern with the abstract concept of justice rather than with the preservation of traditions as sources of law was in Castile, as it had been in Rome, a demonstration of ineffective community integration. A society in which customs can be legally superseded by abstract intellectual ideas is one in which past collective experiences are not usually looked upon as a source of identification and security. Such a pattern of legal organization is indicative of a low degree of social cohesiveness. Adherence to ideal formulas is used as an artificial way of providing the social unity and identification that the institutions of the community do not supply. Search for the ideal is an attempt to integrate and strengthen the society. When a society tries to find ideal patterns of conduct, it could be implicitly admitting the failure, or lack, of traditional ones. Under these circumstances an uncooperative and competitive type of individualism emerges, and the role of the family and the government as providers of safety and security tends to increase.

That Castile was a "new kingdom" did not mean that the communities composing it were devoid of traditions. It meant, however, that local customs could be bypassed in favor of abstract legal formulas and that Castilian communities were probably characterized by uncooperative individualism, escapist idealism, and a closely knit and overprotective family structure.

---

21. Ganivet, *op. cit.*, seems to take a side in this issue when, referring to the mystical character of his compatriots, he asserts: "the Spaniards were Christian before Christ was born." On the influence of Catholic thought on Spanish law see Madden, pp. 65ff.

The lack of correlation between what ought to be and what is, as reflected in the social and psychological patterns of the Roman-Spanish tradition, was transferred to the colonies. The geographic isolation of the new territories helped, if anything, to preserve the unreality of Spanish law. Thus, colonial legislation, as could have been expected, was based on general principles of morality and religion.

As soon as the new lands were discovered, a heated controversy erupted in Spain, and the moral precepts that were to govern the new enterprise were publicly debated. Since it was apparently inconceivable for the country to enact laws for the colonies without a careful evaluation of the problems to be solved, the Crown asked those best qualified to supply the cardinal spiritual and ethical tenets designed to direct the organization of the overseas possessions.[22] The fact that those summoned to the discussion were jurists and theologians shows that the interest centered upon deducing from abstract principles the norms of behavior that people should be admonished to follow. Their recommendations rested upon the sacred ideals of Christianity and aimed at achieving the most desirable forms of ethical conduct. The laws resulting from their advice were highly humanistic and, as the future quickly testified, wholly inoperative.[23]

----

22. For descriptions of the controversy which ensued see Sor M. Mónica, *La gran controversia del siglo XVI acerca del dominio español en América* (Madrid: Ediciones Cultura Hispánica, 1952); and Lewis Hanke, *The Spanish Struggle for Justice in the Conquest of America* (Philadelphia: University of Pennsylvania Press, 1949).

23. Luis Sánchez Agesta, *El concepto del estado en el pensamiento español del siglo XVI* (Madrid: Instituto de Estudios Políticos, 1959), p. 214, affirms that the difference between reality and law in the colonies was actually originated by the philosophical-theological disputes of Las Casas and Vitoria against Sepúlveda

Spanish colonial legislation in general and the famous sixteenth century debate in particular have often been the subjects of scrutiny. The conclusions have varied widely according to whether the examiner paid attention to the letter of the law or to its actual application. Some authors have contended that the laws were enlightened and benign while others have pointed to the abuses and cruelty of the colonists. Both sorts of observers are basically right in their comments although perhaps misguided when they try to evaluate the whole colonial system according to their particular findings. Idealistic royal provisions and constant violation of such orders were present in the colonial system Spain provided for her territories. What should be acknowledged is that such discrepancy between law and reality was no unexplainable development, but rather an intrinsic trait of Spanish legal and social behavior.

A law that is out of tune with the reality it is supposed to regulate is a law that has to be broken. It could be argued that if enough coercive power were available, some "unrealistic" legislation could be enforced. However, even if the logical inconsistency implicit in such an assertion is momentarily overlooked, the fact that an appeal to force was not necessary in the Spanish colonies has to be faced. Violation of the law was anticipated within the legal framework. The repeated disregard of the law by the colonists produced no attempts on the part of

---

and Toledo, and by the need to solve this conflict without violating the principles of the Catholic Church. He goes on to assert that law has always had an artificial character for the Spanish people—that there has been among them a lack of balance between custom and law and that this artificiality of Spanish law should be blamed on too much love for the forms, too much admiration for foreign ideas, and too much willingness to accept dogmatic principles.

the mother country to enforce its application. The lack of physical coercive power at the disposal of the government was one of the most significant aspects of the colonial experience.

So general and widespread was the colonial disregard for the written law that one of the keenest interpreters of the colonial tradition considers any examination of the colonial life based primarily upon the study of written regulations useful only to the extent it detects certain psychological traits of the Spanish people.[24] This persistent violation of the law stand as the source of what Ricardo Levene has called "the characteristic Hispanic American contempt for the law."[25]

The situation that developed in the colonies has been aptly described:

> The carefully written and apparently farseeing decrees, acts, and orders that formed a showcase of minute ingenuity, and which would come one after the other piling up to the size of monuments, would cause the fatigue of scriveners and penmen, would be the delight of pettifoggers, and would nurture the joyful disputes of judges; but Hispanic America would live caring nothing about them. . . . The usual thing was that the royal decrees would be ignored, not only by the Indians, whom the interpreters would notify, but also by the officials themselves. . . . This way of complying with the law has never ceased to be practiced among the people of Hispanic America who so precociously learned it.[26]

24. Juan B. Terán, *El nacimiento de la América española* (Tucumán: Talleres de M. Violetto y Cía., 1927), p. 264.
25. *Notas para el estudio del derecho indiano* (Buenos Aires: Imprenta y Casa Editora "Coví," 1918), pp. 11f.
26. Terán, *op. cit.,* pp. 250f.; see also pp. 153, 247 and 264. On the same subject see Ayarragaray, *op. cit.,* p. 34.

The people from the peninsula and their children, the creoles, exercised control over the social and political life of the colonies which ingrained the attitudes and ideas of the Iberian societies in the new communities. The predominance of Castile in the conquest was an added guarantee to the proper transfusion of Roman-Spanish values. This organization of colonial society along Iberian patterns lends validity, at least from a social and political point of view, to the contention that the differences that were to arise between the English and Spanish colonies in this hemisphere were not merely casual but fundamental.[27]

The Spanish colonization is often summarized as an integrative process of races and cultures. Such a characterization is only partially true and tends to obscure some vital aspects of the colonial experiment. Although there is no doubt that the process of miscegenation began with the arrival of the discoverers, the basic Spanish orientation of the new societies was carefully preserved. A relative attitude of tolerance towards skin pigmentation was accompanied on the part of the Spaniards by a high degree of cultural intolerance. While permissive toward racial integration—an attitude probably explainable in terms of Spanish historical experience—the Spaniards did not hesitate to impose the Iberian system of values upon those who wanted to join their society. Those who did not want, or were not able, to join the white society were usually left alone after their ritualistic conversion to Christianity by means of a quick baptism.

The colonial position with respect to ethnic differences did not spring out of a special sensitivity in the Spanish soul—Spaniards seem to be as open-or close-mind-

27. Bernard Moses, *The Establishment of the Spanish Rule in America* (New York: The Knickerbocker Press, 1907), p. 296.

ed as anyone else—but resulted from their concern with cultural distinctions. Discrimination in the colonies, although not completely divorced from ethnic differences, was not primarily based upon skin color but more upon cultural factors. A nonwhite could, though it was uncommon, be accepted in colonial society only after he had divested himself of his non-Spanish ways. The well-known decrees of *gracias al sacar* that officially changed the color of the skin by virtue of royal sanction represent the Spaniards' attitudes toward races as well as their magical conception of legal power.

New societies fashioned themselves in the image of the mother country and from the conquest on, the colonists tried to be as Spanish as the peninsulars. The physical distance from Spain and the potential hostility of the Indians and the Negroes were factors promoting the desire to identify closely with Europe. In societies where distinctions rested upon modes of behavior rather than on racial classifications, it was important to keep an eye on Spain all the time. The only way of being Spanish was to behave like a Spaniard. Imitation was the order of the day. While the unavoidable process of integration between races and traditions continued to flow within colonial boundaries, the official and intellectual life of the colonies was subjected to the rigid straight jacket of the imitative process. Lack of originality was to be one of the most obvious by-products of such an attitude.

The discrepancy between reality and law was thus retained. The colonies began in fact to feel the influence of their Negro and Indian elements, but the royal institutions would not acknowledge such contacts. Spanish settlers learned from the very beginning to be ashamed of their true ethnic and cultural composition and hid their Negroid and Indian features behind a European mask.

Much of their legal and political histories constituted a ceaseless effort to be what they were not—an effort to make the real conform to the ideal.[28]

The King and the Law

The concept of law that Spain inherited from the Romans was accompanied by a specific interpretation of the royal function. If the goal of the community, as embodied in the law, was to fulfill an ethical principle or perform a spiritual mission, the necessity arose for someone to clarify the scope of the principle and provide leadership for the mission. The implementation of a dogmatically derived rule of conduct implied the need for an interpreter of the dogma, someone who would translate it into specific precepts of behavior. This was the task of the monarch.[29]

In Rome the *officium* of the ruler was to direct the nation in the pursuit of ethical goals that had been dutifully put forward by the philosophers, lawyers, and later on, Fathers of the Church. It was the work of the intellectual theoreticians to investigate the principles of Natural Law and the Christian faith. The responsibility of implementing those principles through rules of conduct—laws—was the *potestas* of the prince.[30]

By thus delegating to the emperor the function of

---

28. See Moreno; *op. cit.* For a most interesting interpretation of the colonizing process see Richard M. Morse, "The Heritage of Latin America," in Louis Hartz (ed.), *The Founding of New Societies* (New York: Harcourt, Brace and World, Inc., 1964), pp. 123ff.
29. Mario Góngora, *El estado en el derecho indiano: época de fundación, 1492–1570* (Santiago: Editorial Universitaria, S. A., 1951), p. 35. In early Roman law this function was, according to Sherman *op. cit.*, Vol. I, pp. 54ff., assigned to the praetor.
30. Sherman, *op. cit.*, Vol. I, pp. 50ff.; and Arangio Ruíz, pp. 267f.

law-maker, the Roman legal thinkers acknowledged his supreme rule while preserving theoretically intact the old structure of power. This was, of course, just one of the legal fictions created by the Roman mind, but one so important that its many implications affected the over-all character of Roman political life. The persistent pre-occupation of the Romans with preserving the forms while violating the substance of old political arrangement repre-sents either the inability of the emperors to make the reality of the imperial government acceptable or the hope that by retaining in form the traditional institutions, the actual political situation would conform to them. Both alternatives were in fact expressions of the same es-capist tendencies and as such were closely interrelated.

Through the use of ideal formulas the emperors at-tempted to legitimize their power. Those who acquired power through violent means would always promptly ex-plain their actions in terms of ethical principles. The flexibility of a law that emanated from abstract con-cept of justice allowed the emperors to claim loyalty to the republican precepts while they ruled according to their own will. In such a fashion, dictatorial rule walked hand in hand with judicial idealism through the history of the mighty empire.

Early Christian writers well understood that actual power lay with the emperor and took care to assure the rulers of the empire that their Church was not after their earthly might and that its function was limited to pro-viding spiritual counsel and moral advice.[31] A similar theoretical conception of political power was to be found in the Iberian peninsula. Here the Christian monarch claimed total control in the name of God and the pursuit

31. The writings of St. Paul, St. Ambrose, St. Augustine, and St. Gregory offer ample example of this attitude.

of justice. In the performance of the royal *officium,* he relied upon Christian dogma and his sense of equity. His duty was to promote the common good which, once translated into Christian terms, meant the salvation of the soul.[32]

As had been the case with the Roman praetor[33] and emperor, the Spanish monarch through his appeal to ethics enjoyed a position above the law. It was the royal function to determine, in the name of Christian justice, the law of the land. As it had been said of the Roman emperor, it could equally be said of the Spanish king: *"Qua quod principi placuit legis habet vigorem"* (What pleases the prince has the force of law). The will of the Spanish monarch ruled supreme over the customs and the traditions of the ancient communities and the ways of the people came to be considered of lesser spiritual and moral, and therefore legal, value than the edicts of the king.[34]

The establishment of the monarch's law-giving function was coordinated with the introduction of a legal fiction that vested upon the ruler a dual legal and political personality. In his actions as an individual, the king was, like everyone else, subject to the canons of private law. As the maker of the law and in his capacity as a public legal institution, the king was meant to be honest and impartial with only the interest of the public in mind. Because he was ruling for the common good in a Christian, just, and equitable manner, the monarch deserved absolute loyalty: to disobey him was to go against

---

32. Madden, *op. cit.,* pp. 19ff., and pp. 101f.
33. "The Roman praetor, unlike the judge of modern times, was not subject to the law; he was superior to it." Sherman, *op. cit.,* Vol. I, p. 54.
34. Góngora, *op. cit.,* p. 21.

the will of God.[35] The consistency and the purity of ideal thinking were wholly maintained by rendering fealty to the king's office or *ministerium* and not to the man occupying it.

This duality was sanctioned by the Roman artificial distinction between public and private law. The relationship of the state, when acting in its governmental capacity, with its subjects, is the realm of public law. The relationship between the subjects themselves, or between the subjects and the state, when the latter is acting in a non-governmental capacity, constitutes the realm of private law.[36]

At the same time that the king was entrusted with these public responsibilities, the fictional legal formula anticipated that as an individual, that is, in his private law capacity, he would not misuse the powers of his office. In other words, the ruler was expected to act simultaneously in two capacities, without mixing them or allowing one to influence the actions of the other. As a private individual, the king was to be subject to the laws he himself had enacted as a public official.[37] The unreality of

---

35. Since the monarch was ruling in the name of God and in the performance of his *officium* or *ministerium,* this obedience developed into a divine right of the king. See José Deleito y Piñuela, *El declinar de la monarquía española* (Madrid: Espasa-Calpe, S. A., 1955), p. 35; Henry S. Maine, *Ancient Law* (London: Oxford University Press, 1931. First published in 1861), p. 287; and Sabine, *op. cit.,* p. 182.

36. For a discussion of the Roman law conception of private and public law and of some of its implications, see J. Walter Jones, *Historical Introduction to the Theory of Law* (London: Oxford University Press, 1956. First published in 1940), pp. 139ff.

37. Arangio Ruíz, *op. cit.,* pp. 267ff., points to a similar duality in the case of the Roman emperor symbolized in the term *auctoritas* and *potestas.* This duality can still be easily seen in the contemporary Spanish and Latin American legal systems where the governmental institutions may act with either a private or a public law personality.

this supposition was increased by the fact that the Spanish monarch claimed actual ownership of his kingdoms.

These fine legal distinctions amounted to little in practice. The duality prescribed by the judicial abstractions could not alter the biological unity of the royal person. For all practical purposes, the king enjoyed a position of privilege with respect to the law since as it has been appropriately stated, "he who establishes the law is not subject to it."[38] If anything, the inoperative distinction between the public and private law spheres of royal action helped lay the foundations for absolute monarchy in the name of justice.

As a Catholic ruler in the performance of his *officium,* the king of Spain became the "executor of the divine will" subject only to "the laws of God and nature."[39] It was for him to decide what the best interest of his people required on every occasion and how to bring justice and happiness to his nation.[40] The moral, legal, and political powers ascribed to the office were conducive to the idealization of the Crown, and under certain circumstances, of the person wearing it.

Any attempt to modify a situation through the enactment of legislation required royal sanction. And an idealistic conception of the role of law could not persist without an idealistic understanding of the royal function. If law was thought of as possessing redeeming qualities,

---

38. Andrés Mano, *El príncipe perfecto* as quoted in Deleito, *op. cit.,* p. 25f. This was also the opinion of St. Thomas Aquinas.
39. Pedro de Ribadeneyra, *El príncipe cristiano* (Buenos Aires: Editorial Sopena Argentina, S.C., 1942. First published in 1595), p. 33. See also Deleito, *op. cit.,* p. 34.
40. It is interesting to note that St. Augustine and St. Isidore had both stated that happiness was not possible in this world. The king was not then expected to be greatly concerned with the material wellbeing of his subjects.

the maker of the law was potentially a redeemer and so looked upon by those whose destinies rested in his hands. Their major political concern was not the slow process of finding specific answers to exact questions, but rather the ability or willingness of the rulers to use the power of their office. Those who lived convinced of the almost magical powers at the disposal of the monarch could not but build their hopes and expectations on his actions. People would not consider a given porblem on the basis of whether or not it could be solved, but—most problems being theoretically solvable by the king—on the basis of whether or not he was willing to do so.[41] Royal power came to be considered omnipotent. An exaggerated concern with the will of the ruler rather than with an objective evaluation of the office's potential became an inevitable concomitant of such political beliefs.

Castile was the first Spanish kingdom in which this concept of monarchical rule was successfully developed. The idea of the Crown as law-maker and supreme political institution is distinctly stated in the laws of *Las Siete Partidas* (1256–1265). The king of Castile was soon enacting a new kind of legislation in the form of ordinances and decrees. These executive actions gained force of law "at first by means of Parliamentary ratification and later despite the complaints of Parliament."[42]

The will of the king became the highest source of

---

41. Sebastian de Grazia, *The Political Community: A Study of Anomie* (Chicago: The University of Chicago Press. First Phoenix Edition, 1963), p. 22, sees this Messianic function as proper of all political rule: "for a person is not a *ruler* no matter how powerful the forces at his command, unless the members of the community believe in his capacity and willingness to guide and provide for them."

42. Góngora, *op. cit.,* p. 28. This early executive supremacy could be helpful in explaining the Latin American tendency to legislate by means of *decretos* and *decretos-leyes.*

law throughout the country. The Castilian monarchy departed from tradition in civil and penal legislation, intervened in religious disputes, and confirmed its dynastic independence, all of which proved that the monarch had become the major source of law and authority. By the thirteenth century, the principle of absolute royal control was well established in Castile.[43] The eventual predominance of Castile over the rest of the Spanish kingdoms assured the success of such a concept of royal power all over Spain, although being already familiar to other kingdoms, it might well have prevailed even without Castile's influence.

Authoritism

Under the Roman-Spanish legal and political concept of authority, the ruler held a position above the law (*Lex* or *Ley*), and in the performance of his functions he enjoyed almost unlimited powers. On the other hand, the monarch was operating within a system of law (*Ius* or *Derecho*). That is, his ample powers and prerogatives were legitimate according to the prevailing legal-political formula. The general tendency has been to classify the role played by the Spanish Crown as authoritarian. But such classification, unless properly qualified, is highly misleading. The term authoritarian implies some element of illegitimacy, and its application to the Spanish colonial system has obscured the fact that royal predominance was psychologically accepted and legally sanctioned.

The mixture of absolute power with the acceptance of such power seems to defy usual classifications. In their accepted usage neither authority nor authoritarianism

---

43. *Ibid.*, p. 29; and John Lynch, *Spain under the Habsburgs* (New York: Oxford University Press, 1964), Vol. I, p. 8.

would fit the Spanish political equation. The former conveys the idea of power under the law in the traditional Anglo-Saxon way, and the latter suggests illegitimacy. Therefore, in order to facilitate the comprehension of some of the relationships and attitudes present in the Spanish colonial system a new term will be used. *Authoritism* will be understood as the existence of a single center of legitimate political power, the legal supremacy of which is sanctioned in the name of justice and whose actions are, therefore, not to be bound by written regulations or existing customs.

We now can say that the Spanish political system was not authoritarian but authoritistic—a term of greater descriptive value to the case in question. Application of the term authoritistic would remind observers that Spanish royal supremacy was accepted and will help to stress this acceptance.

According to our newly developed definition, the Roman and Spanish empires present some very substantial differences in their political structure. The elements of acceptance and legitimacy so vital to authoritism seem to have been largely absent in Rome. At present, of course, it would be foolish to try to determine with accuracy the degree of acceptance enjoyed by each empire, but the relative stability present in each case would provide some general guidelines for an overall estimate. And if stability is defined as the continuity of legal forms and the absence of spurious military control over governmental affaris, it would have to be concluded and whereas the Spanish empire during the sixteenth, seventeenth, and eighteenth centuries was highly stable, the Roman imperial system was almost constantly plagued with instability.

The fortunes of the Roman empire fluctuated according to the strength and weaknesses of the individual rulers. A resourceful military leader or a shrewd politician could retain control of the empire for some time, but even if he managed to survive the ambitions of the military and the machinations of the praetorian guards and court officials, once he died the problem of establishing a stable rule would have to be faced by his successors. Political stability in Rome was usually short-lived and only rarely would it survive the leader responsible for its attainment. Although the Romans developed an abstract conception intended to direct loyalty toward the office and not the person of the ruler, they seem to have been unable to put it into effect during the latter part of the republic and empire. At best, they were able to use loyalty to a leader, charisma, as a legitimizing element.

In contrast to the Roman experience, loyality in the Castilian kingdom, from the time of Fernando and Isabel, seems to have been directed toward the institution of monarchy rather than toward the person of the monarch. Thus, the stability of the system was not dependent upon the ability of a given individual to control governmental institutions or public will, or both. The Romans fluctuated between authoritarianism and authoritism based upon charisma, but the Spaniards seem to have been successful in creating institutional authoritism. The authoritarian, or dictatorial, Roman system was undermined by its inability to elicit acceptance; and personal, or charismatic, authoritism could only be a temporary legitimizing device.

The difference between personal and institutional authoritism could also be explained in Max Weber's terminology by stating that the Roman one was basically charismatic while the Spanish one was traditional. Weber explains charismatic authority as "resting on devotion to the specific and exceptional sanctity, heroism or exemplary character of an individual person, and of the nominative patterns or order revealed or ordained by him." He considers traditional authority as that "resting on an established belief in the sanctity of immemorial traditions."[44]

It is very important to keep in mind that systems based upon charismatic or traditional authority are accepted as legitimate. Their existence and operation are justified through a legal formula that is expressed in cultural and psychological terms understood by the nations in question. Therefore, authoritistic rule, personal as well as institutional, must be distinguished from illegitimate government that has failed to justify its existence in terms that are acceptable to the population under its control. There could be many different variations of illegitimate rule. An illegitimate government could be absolutistic or self-limited in the amount of power it claims, and the degree of its monistic or pluralistic structure could differ greatly from case to case. What all illegitimate systems share in common is a basic, latent instability stemming from their inability to have their claims to legitimacy accepted.[45]

Needless to say, there could be great similarities between some forms of illegitimate and legitimate government. A monistic and absolutistic illegitimate rule could structurally resemble very closely a system of personal authoritism. The major difference between them would be their potential for attaining stability. While the power

---

44. Max Weber, *The Theory of Social and Economic Organization.* Translated by A. M. Henderson and Talcott Parsons (New York: The Free Press, 1964), p. 328.
45. The determination, within a given country, of whose consent is needed for the legitimization of a political system is necessary if we are to understand its political life.

of the former would rest on its ability to control and manipulate instruments of physical coercion, the ultimate power of the latter would be rooted in public allegiance.[46] Illegitimate dictatorship, based on naked power, would exist in constant peril, while personal authoritistic rule, relying on the acceptance of its claim to legitimacy, would tend to enjoy better chances of survival.[47]

Furthermore, it must be realized that these systems are not necessarily static or the difference between them constant. An illegitimate system could, under certain circumstances, become a legitimate one. For example, a dictatorial government whose only initial source of power is force could evolve into a system of personal authoritism; or a legitimate rule based on charisma could, after some internal adjustment, shift its legitimacy claims to traditional grounds.

The definitions and distinctions that have been presented so far require further analysis and interpretations. But while recognizing this need to deal in more detail with their theoretical and practical implications, the evaluation of their effect upon the Spanish colonial system will be attempted.

Spanish Institutional Authoritism

Spain, after the reign of Isabel and Fernando, came to enjoy a system of government whose claim to legitimacy was widely accepted. This is especially true after the last municipal revolts against royal power had been put down.

46. On the relationship between allegiance and authority see Harold D. Lasswell and Abraham Kaplan, *Power and Society: A Framework for Political Inquiry* (New Haven: Yale University Press, 1950), p. 134.
47. It is necessary to remember that we are not here considering only individual tenure of office, but the chances for survival of the system's legal and institutional foundations.

During the sixteenth century, clear signs that loyalty was rendered more to the royal office (*ministerium*) than to the person of the monarch can be detected. The legal ideas inherited from Rome providing for such an interpretation of royal authority cannot be taken, by itself, as the cause for its actual coming into existence. The same legal formula failed to bring about a similar development in Rome, and it had also been unsuccessful in the Spanish kingdoms for several centuries. Thus, there could be little doubt that there were particular elements in fifteenth century Spain that made possible the creation of institutional authoritism. Without going into the specific circumstances conducive to such a development, its most vital functional characteristics can be isolated.

The Spanish monarch acted within a system of *derecho* but without, in practice, being subject to the *ley*. The term *derecho* describes the general system of law, including its ideological and philosophical aspects; the word *ley* means enacted legislation. Whereas the Anglo-Saxon ruler was bound, by the customs and traditions (laws) of his community, to the extent exemplified in the famous dictum, "the king is only king under the law," his Spanish counterpart enjoyed an absolutistic and monistic authority that was not considered extra-legal, but quite to the contrary, most compatible with the overall system of law.

The acceptance by the Spaniards of political authoritism could be seen as indicative of certain social, psychological, and cultural trends. Although this is not the place to try to determine the exact relationship between such traits and the establishment of authoritistic rule, it must be admitted that the success of such a political scheme implies the existence, latent or expressed, of a certain inclination toward absolutistic and monistic organization. A conception of political order alien to the

nation could hardly enjoy any chances of being legitimized.[48] If political behavior is the way in which a social
group approaches a certain category of problems, and if
the human mind is integrative,[49] it would logically follow
that the political responses of a community must somehow be in accord with its psychological composition and
patterns of social expression.

Our knowledge of Spanish and colonial society indicates receptivity to a system of government that was in
many ways modeled along the lines of traditional paternal
authority. The stability of Spanish institutional authoritism should not be attributed as much to any intrinsic
quality of the system as to the fact that this form of political organization must have coincided with the inclinations
and expectancies of those who were ruled by it. [50]

---

48. The necessity for the political scheme to be consistent with
    other cultural factors could be well understood if we accept
    Talcott Parson's idea "that cultural elements are elements of
    patterned order which mediate and regulate communication
    and other aspects of the mutuality of orientations in interac-
    tion processes." (*The Social System*. New York: The Free Press
    1946), p. 327.
49. On the integrative character of the human mind see Abram
    Kardiner, *The Psychological Frontiers of Society* (New York:
    Columbia University Press, 1963. First published in 1945), p.
    421.
50. Cecil Jane, *Liberty and Despotism in Spanish America*. (Lon-
    don: Oxford University Press, 1929), p. 43, describes the suc-
    cess of the Spanish colonial systems as follows: "Until the early
    years of the nineteenth century Spain ruled her American pos-
    sessions with the free consent and goodwill of their inhabitants.
    That consent and goodwill was not the outcome of gratitude
    for material benefits received or for the intellectual advantages
    conferred; it was not tribute to the excellent organization of
    the government, and it can hardly be regarded as the result of
    fear of the coercive power of the court of Madrid. It seems, in
    fact, that the peculiar administrative system established a sys-
    tem which was hardly a system at all, satisfying, during the
    greater part of the period for which endured, the temperament

The King as a Moderating Power

Since it was the task of the monarch, under the authoritistic organization of power, to rule for the common good, impartially, and in the name of justice, he came to be considered what in Rome Cicero had called the *moderator republicae*.[51] As the God-appointed maker of the law and the provider of justice, the king came to be looked upon as a mediating or moderating force. This expectancy was reflected in the legal formula that assigned to him the role of arbiter among conflicting interests, groups, and individuals composing the kingdom.

The dual legal personality possessed by the monarch made juridically possible the implementation of his moderating function. In his public capacity the king ruled in the name of justice for the benefit of the kingdom. As an institution of public law the Crown was a paternalistic symbol to which all those seeking the redress of some grievance or merely wanting protection of their interests could appeal for help. In his pursuit of justice and the public good the Spanish monarch could overrule any law, statute, or custom. It was even expected that he would change, reform, amend, or annul any of the actions he himself, or any other functionary, might have taken in the past if they conflicted with the primary royal obligation—equitable rule.

The king as a moderator could hear petitions against actions he had taken as head of the administrative apparatus. This situation was further facilitated by the kingdoms

of the Spanish race and of those who were imbued with Spanish ideas."

51. *The Republic,* Fifth Book. The moderating capacity of the Spanish monarch has been mentioned by several writers although no one, to my knowledge, has dealt with it specifically or at length. See Deleito, *op. cit.,* pp. 28f.; and Góngora,, *op. cit.,* p. 26.

being considered patrimonial property of the Crown.[52] In the laws for the colonies, the title of *señor* was specifically vested upon the monarch;[53] thus the relationship between the king and his subjects had strong feudal elements. The distinction between royal functions and the patrimonial property of the king had been well established in Castile beginning in the thirteenth century.[54] Like other Castilian legal and political institutions of Roman origin, this one was also present in the neighboring Spanish kingdoms.

The operational outgrowth of the royal moderating function was the introduction into the system of an apparent element of flexibility. If a tribunal of justice, or an administrative council, or the monarch himself took an action that adversely affected someone, the affected party could always appeal, in the name of ethical principles, for redress to the king in his moderating capacity. Since the accepted goal of the system was the attainment of justice, all those who felt justice was not being done were justified in appealing to the Crown. Such appeals, or the ability or right to make them, became in this way a stabilizing factor in the system of royal supremacy. Although the monarch held absolute political authority, his

---

52. The Hispanic American territories were considered the patrimonial property of the Crown. On this subject see Ricardo Levene, *Las Indias no eran colonias* (Buenos Aires: Espasa-Calpe Argentina, S.A., 1951); José Martínez Cardos, "Las Indias y las Cortes de Castilla durante los siglos XVI y XVII," in *Revista de Indias,* year XVI, number 64 (April-June 1956), pp. 207ff.; and year XVI, number 65 (July-September 1956), pp. 357ff.; Juan Manzano, *La incorporación de las Indias a la corona de Castilla* (Madrid: Ediciones Cultura Hispánica, 1948), pp. 300ff.; Góngora, *op. cit.,* pp. 36ff.; and Raúl Carrancá y Trujillo, *La evolución política de Iberoamérica* (Madrid: Editorial Reus, 1925), p. 44.
53. *Recopilación . . . ., op. cit.,* Libro III, Título I, Ley 1a.
54. Góngora., *op. cit.,* p. 18.

claim to it was supported by his commitment to allow challenges to its use that he, the monarch, would hear and rule upon. Individual initiative had to be channeled through the moderating capacity of the Crown and thus depended upon the acceptance of royal supremacy.

As the head of the royal administrative machinery, the king provided for a detailed structure of power and for a specific chain of command. In practice, however, disagreement with his actions could be expressed by anyone to him.[55] The legal duality was thus politically institutionalized, and the complex pyramid of hierarchical power was undermined by a direct link between the king and his subjects.

The ability of the subjects to appeal to the monarch in the name of justice was one of the ingredients directly responsible for the effectiveness of the system. If the actual royal dispositions, in accord with the idealistic conception of law, frequently tended to be unrealistic, it was clear that on many occasions they were not, or could not, be obeyed. Under different circumstances, such disobedience would have provoked an open clash with the Crown and would have constituted a threat to royal authority. But under the accepted concept of royal rule and by means of the monarch's moderating function, the legal dispositions enacted by the Crown did not possess a final and inflexible character. It could safely be stated that under such circumstances lack of compliance with royal enactments could easily be tolerated since it constituted a reaffirmation of loyalty to the basic nature of the system.

In the colonies the situation was generally the same

---

55. Theoretically, everyone in the colonies had the right to complain to Madrid. In practice, however, there were vast differences between the ability of different groups and individuals to make use of this right.

as in Spain; the royal officials could choose between accepting the orders coming from Madrid or appealing to the king. Voicing loyalty to the Crown, they could fail to comply with the laws and regulations enacted by the monarch. John L. Phelan in his examination of the colonial system explains this phenomenon in terms of the "conflicting standard analysis" approach.[56] He asserts that the Spanish officials in the colonies were faced with a variety of standards they could enforce. They were given a choice that not only produced a certain degree of flexibility toward the application of royal orders but also promoted greater dependence upon the Crown. Phelan's conclusion becomes remarkably enlightening when seen in terms of the moderating capacity of the Crown.

The actual flexibility, or the discretionary power that the colonial officials enjoyed, had only, of course, a suspensive character. The representatives of the Crown in the colonies could refuse the application of a given royal disposition but, not being able to legislate for themselves, they could only request from the king new or modified regulations.[57] Actual disobedience implicitly reaffirmed dependence on the king. Such a concept of royal power should illuminate some of the social and psychological characteristics of colonial life. Loyalty to an absolute ruler was coupled with actual disregard for royal orders. Within this combination of dependence and independence, some

---

56. "Authority and Flexibility in the Spanish Imperial Bureaucracy" in the *Administrative Science Quarterly,* Vol. I (June 1960), pp. 47ff. This approach was originally developed by Andrew G. Frank, "Goal Ambiguity and Conflicting Standards: An Approach to the Study of Organization," in *Human Organization,* Vol. 17, No. 4, (1958–1959), pp. 8ff., in a study of the Russian industrial bureaucracy.

57. José M. Ots Capdequi, *El estado español en las Indias* (México: Fondo de Cultura Económica, 1957), pp. 62f.

of the mechanisms that permitted the functioning of the system for over three hundred years without major difficulty can be distinguished.[58]

Se Acata Pero No Se Cumple

The compound of flexibility and dependence prescribed in the political formula was explicitly stated in the *se acata pero no se cumple* legal device.[59] This Spanish juridical institution enabled colonial officials to disregard the laws enacted in Madrid by appealing to the king, that is, by reaffirming their allegiance to the Crown. The direct relationship between the monarch and his subjects, which was a requisite for the moderating function of the ruler, was thus sanctioned. It was as if a father were to grant his children the privilege of disobeying those of his orders which they thought unjust, promising them that once he was informed he would reevaluate them in

---

58. Some authors maintain that the deterioration of the Spanish monarchy actually began with the establishment in Spain of the Bourbon dynasty in 1700. Some of them go so far as to see in the weakening of the authoritarian-theological tradition of the Hapsburgs, the real cause of the loss of the colonies. For an example of the latter see José Coronel Urtecho as quoted by Marius André, *El fin del imperio español en América* (Barcelona: Editorial Araluce, 1939). Jane, *op. cit.*, pp. 81ff., sees the wars of independence as protests against the anti-Spanish measures of the Bourbon reforms. In any event, it is interesting to note that it was under the Bourbons that the need for a military establishment was first felt in the colonies. See Edwin Lieuwen, *Arms and Politics in Latin America* (New York: Frederick A. Praeger, Publisher, 1961), p. 18; and William S. Stokes, *Latin American Politics* (New York: Thomas Y. Crowell Co., 1959), p. 108.

59. The verb *obedecer* is sometimes used instead of *acatar,* the sentence then reading *se obedece pero no se cumple.* In this context both verbs have the same meaning. The translation of this sentence should read: "The law is accepted but not complied with."

the interest of love and justice. The colonial children had in the king an understanding father always willing to forgive their disobedience, but whose same forgiveness precluded the development of a sense of responsibility on the part of the children.[60]

This peculiar institution was stated in the laws of the Indies as follows:

> Ministers and judges should obey but not comply with our decrees and orders in which the vices of obreption and subreption have intervened, and at the first opportunity should inform us as to reasons why they did not do it.[61]

The Crown, by this disposition, explicitly acknowledged the right of its subjects to disregard the written law when they thought the king had lacked the necessary elements for arriving at a just and equitable decision. The idealistic character of the law was in this way reinforced, the duality between law and reality preserved, and the authoritistic character of the monarchy safeguarded. Under such a system there was little opportunity for the colonists to develop antagonistic feelings toward the prince. For all intents and purposes he removed himself from their way. The colonists were allowed to do much of what they wanted at the seemingly low price of periodically renewing their allegiance to the Crown.

The working of this institution and its consequences have been described in the following way:

---

60. Spanish writers tend to explain the development of this institution in terms of the wisdom and liberalism of the Crown. See Vicente D. Sierra, *Así se hizo América* (Madrid: Editores Cultura Hispánica, 1955), p. 134; and Carmelo Viñas Mey, "La organización administrativa de España en América," in *Cultura Hispanoamericana,* year IV, number 103 (June 1921), p. 10.
61. *Recopilación. . . . , op. cit.,* Libro II, Título I, Ley xxij.

No chief, or judge, or municipal council did ever fail to offer submission to the royal words, "after they were kissed and put over the head" of the darkest royal official, in the remotest Hispanic American hamlet. With ceremonious acknowledgement they swore to obey the supreme order, but the laws were never carried out when the slightest passion or interest was an obstacle to it. This phenomenon founded an extraordinary school of ingenuity and dialectics, of hypocrisy and disobedience. The arguments were prompt, proud and elegant, sometimes even eloquent, all of them based on the better service of "his royal, holy, Catholic and Caesarean Majesty."[62]

The *se acata pero no se cumple* principle was the embodiment of some of the most fundamental characteristics of Spanish institutional authoritism. This institution cannot be considered as an isolated peculiarity of the colonial organization, but must be seen as the actual reflection of the dual concept of law, and of the moderating attributes of the Crown. Through this device, the king gave royal sanction to the disobedience of his laws in return for allegiance to his moderating power, which in fact, meant to the system. Politically, there were reasons for all parties involved to agree on it. The colonial officials could exercise a high degree of discretion within an acceptable legal formula, while the monarch was able, without the use of force, to keep the empire together.[63]

---

62. Terán, *op. cit.*, pp. 254f. See also J. H. Parry, *The Spanish Theory of Empire in the Sixteenth Century* (London: Cambridge University Press, 1940), p. 74; and C. H. Haring, *The Spanish Empire in America* (New York: Oxford University Press, 1947), p. 123.

63. As basic as a good knowledge of the *se acata pero no se cumple* principle is to the proper understanding of the colonial system, there seems to be no available study of it. There is no

The smooth operation of the colonial system for so many years is less difficult to comprehend if we understand the colonial attitude toward law and political authority. The lack of internal order that plagued the life of the colonies did not conflict with the uninterrupted loyalty to Spain. The disregard for reality, characteristic of Spanish legal thinking, created an almost anarchical domestic situation that was sanctioned by allegiance to a paternalistic symbol representing the highest possible moral and spiritual values. Law (*ley*) in the colonies became a lay catechism that, as its spiritual counterpart, was to be praised in theory and violated in practice.

The Role of the Crown in the Colonies

No attempt to envision colonial politics would be worthwhile without a detailed analysis of the function performed by the Spanish Crown in the new world since, according to the authoritistic formula, the Spanish king was the center of all colonial political life. By the time Columbus arrived in America, the developmental process

book on Latin American government and politics, or history, which, to my knowledge, concerns itself with the nature and implications of this Spanish legal device or with the political ideas and attitudes that made it possible. Only a very small number of Latin American writers have dealt at any length with the character of this institution and/or with the political and sociopsychological forces that gave it birth. See Agustín Alvarez, *South America: ensayo de psicología política* (Buenos Aires: La Cultura Argentina, 1918); Lucas Ayarragaray, *Estudios históricos, políticos y literarios* (Buenos Aires: Talleres Gráficos Argentinos L. J. Rosso, 1936); Lucas Ayarragaray, *La anarquia . . . , op. cit.*; Luis Alberto Sánchez, *¿Existe América Latina?* (México: Fondo de Cultura Económica, 1945); Laureano Vallenilla Lanz, *Cesarismo democrático* (Fourth Edition; Caracas: Tipografía Garrido, 1961) ; Juan Bautista Alberdi, *Las bases* (Buenos Aires: Librería La Facultad, 1915); and Juan B. Terán,, *op. cit.*

of royal authoritism was almost complete in Spain. Castile had become the most powerful kingdom of the peninsula and with the marriage of Fernando and Isabel the final act in the integration of Spain under Castilian domination had begun. The absolute supremacy of the monarch was consolidated under the Hapsburg kings.[64]

Institutional authoritism was exported to the colonies with the other Castilian beliefs and customs. Colonial officials were assigned specific and often detailed functions, and a vertical chain of command was established that went from the king to the last colonial official. This formal organization resembled a pyramid of power with the king at the apex, but in practice, however, the system showed a different shape. The king, in his paternalistic role of moderating power, was able to communicate with everyone directly, in complete disregard of the pyramidal organization prescribed by the legislation. Any colonial subject or institution desiring to approach the Crown could do so in the name of justice. Thus, the hierarchy of power never really functioned. The direct links established between the king and his subjects made it inoperative. The actual structure of the Spanish colonial system was that of a center, the Crown, around which the institutional life of the colonies was arranged. "The organization of political power in the Indies did not have the configuration of a pyramid but it could be better compared to a circle whose radii come all from the

---

64. On the development of the powers of the king see Góngora, *op. cit.*, pp. 15ff.; and Juan Beneyto Pérez, *Historia de la administración española e hispanoamericana* (Madrid: Aguilar, S.A. de Ediciones, 1958); and Jesús de Galíndez, *Iberoamérica: su evolución política, socio-económica, cultural e internacional* (New York: Las Américas Publishing Co., 1954), pp. 61f. For a description of the decline of the powers of the Hapsburgs see Deleito, *op. cit.*

Crown."[65] Or as John A. Crow simply stated: "all the strings went back to Madrid."[66]

The lack of coordination between the real and the legal rendered the official structure of power inoperative. Therefore, the actual life of the colonial institutions can only be understood, not in terms of the position they were assigned by law, but rather by their true relations with the Crown.

Internal Struggle for Power

Direct dependence upon the king acted as a leveling force among colonial institutions. The direct accessibility to the monarch enjoyed by all the colonists supplied the basis for the permanent internal struggle for power that characterized the lives of the Spanish colonial possessions. For all practical purposes, the different colonial institutions came to be almost completely independent of each other. John Lynch's definition of government in the peninsula could be properly applied to the colonies: "the method of government was personal monarchy exercised through centralized but not unified institutions."[67]

Or as Ricardo Zorraquín Becú has more explicitly observed:

> There did not exist a strict dependence between the different institutions and functionaries. On the contrary, everybody acted within his sphere, although supervised by everybody else. For example, the vice-

---

65. Ricardo Zorraquín Becú, *La organización política argentina en el período hispánico* (Second Edition; Buenos Aires: Editorial Perrot, 1962), p. 57. Deleito, *op. cit.,* p. 46 believes this structural pattern to be characteristic of all absolute monarchies.
66. *The Epic of Latin America* (New York: Doubleday and Co., Inc., 1946), p. 167.
67. Lynch, *op. cit.,* p. 47.

roy would give orders to the governor but the governor had usually been appointed directly by the king and would communicate directly with him. The Council of Indies would also give orders to the governor without going through the viceroy and sometimes without even informing him. The ordinances dictated by the governor would not go to the viceroy for confirmation but to the Council of Indies. . . . Each authority was dependent upon one and, although having a certain functional autonomy, could be controlled by institutions that were not actually its superiors. It was a system of ductile hierarchy which showed its efficiency in its flexibility.[68]

The actual distribution of power contained in the laws of the Indies was, at its best, an effort to describe the ideal relationship that should exist among the colonial officials themselves, and between them and the Crown. In practice, however, every institution struggled to acquire as much power as its ability and circumstances would permit. Feeling no compulsion to adhere to the formal hierarchical structure, the colonial institutions lived in the midst of a continuous battle for control and supremacy.

Internal domination was usually the result of a favorable balance of forces within the colony, but royal consent or approval was a most important element in the colonial conflict for power, and thus a coveted goal of the interests at play. A favorable royal decree, although carrying no guarantee of being implemented, would tend to enhance the prestige and improve the position of the favored party. It would seem somehow contradictory that those same people who would not hesitate to violate the

---

68. Zorraquín, *op. cit.,* p. 57.

law could be concerned with it in any way, but such a rationale would lead to gross oversimplification. As Max Weber has explained:

> It is possible for action to be oriented to an order in other ways than through conformity with its prescriptions, as they are generally understood by the actors. Even in the cases of evasion or deliberate disobedience to these prescriptions, the probability of its being recognized as a valid norm may have an effect on action.[69]

Though Spanish law was usually unreal, in a common law sense, it did not lack importance. In a system where actual freedom of action was so intimately related to formal obedience, the colonists developed an active concern for working in accordance with the accepted principles. To this must be added the fact that not all Spanish laws were ineffective or inconsequential. Guided by the almost magical qualities they attributed to the written law, some colonists would look upon royal edicts as capable of molding reality and their eventual failure to do so was blamed, not on the monarchy or the system, but on the interference of ill-disposed officials.

The most influential political institutions of the colonies were the viceroy or governor, the *audiencia*, the *cabildo*, and the Church.[70] The spheres of power, ad-

---

69. Weber, *op. cit.,.p.* 125.
70. In classifying the Catholic Church as a political institution, I am following the advice of Charles H. Cunningham, *The Audiencia in the Spanish Colonies as Illustrated by the Audiencia of Manila* (Berkeley: University of California Press, 1919), p. 3. Diffie, *op. cit.,* pp. 284ff., also sees four centers of political power: throne, clergy, aristocracy, and municipalities. His interpretation is in basic harmony with mine since the aristocracy in the colonies was usually identified with either the *audiencia* or the *cabildo* according to their peninsular or creole origin.

ministrative duties, and general jurisdiction of these colonial institutions and their officials were, in practice, confused and there was a great deal of functional duplication. When a strong and able viceroy or governor was at the helm of the colonial government, he could manage to make his will prevail through the effective use of his executive office and his contacts in Madrid, but once this force was removed, the colonies would relapse into their characteristic internal institutional struggle.

This interminable contest, which frequently took violent form, became an integral part of the Spanish colonial system of government. The more the colonial officials disputed among themselves, the more interested they were in securing royal support, and thus the more intensive was their concern with proving their loyalty to the Crown. Historians have tended to neglect the symbolic significance of the commonly used colonial battle cry: *¡Viva el Rey! ¡Muera el mal gobierno!* (Long live the king! Death to bad government!) The use of this slogan reflected the nature and mechanics of the system and it clearly represented the dependency of colonial power upon the acceptance of the authoritistic principle.

The viceroys engaged in almost daily conflicts with the Church, the *audiencia,* and the *cabildo.* The members of the *audiencia* quarreled among themselves and with everyone else. The *cabildos* experienced frequent clashes with all the other colonial institutions. And the Church divided its time almost equally between internal and external conflicts. All these disputes were reflected in the colonial correspondence to the monarch and their description has provided enough material for historians to

---

What Diffie calls throne can easily be identified with the viceroy or captain-general, who was the direct representative of the king's executive power.

fill many pages.[71] The political life of colonial Hispanic America could be understood in terms of the innumerable written and personal pleas to the Crown.[72]

Whatever other features the Spanish colonists developed in America during the three hundred years of colonial rule, their loyalty to the Crown, in an institutional authoritistic form, remained basically unaltered. As Frank Tannenbaum has said, "whatever criticism might be made against the government—that it was foolish, cruel, or stupid, for example—the symbol of authority remained sacred."[73] Internal conflict and allegiance to the Crown were the two fundamental political characteristics of the colonial period.

71. This situation is interpreted by Phelan, *op cit.*, as follows: "The existence of multiple hierarchies and alternate channels of communications prevents subordinates from obstructing the upward movement of information. By providing superiors with a wide fund of knowledge about conditions below, subordinates are made more responsible to their superiors." On the ability of the colonists to approach the Crown directly see Zorraquín, *op. cit.*, p. 59.
72. Ots, *op. cit.*, p. 56. In spite of the great amount of available material, no systematic and detailed study of this power struggle is, to my knowledge, on record.
73. *Ten Keys to Latin America* (New York: Alfred A. Knopf, 1962), p. 67. See also Salvador de Madariaga, "El ocaso del imperio español en América" in *El Ciclo Hispánico* (Buenos Aires: Editorial Sudamericana, 1958), Vol. II, p. 223; and Harold Davis (ed.), *Government and Politics in Latin America* (New York: The Ronald Press, 1958), p. 124.

The Political Organization of Colonial Chile

The Spanish colonial system was organized around a highly idealized monistic interpretation of political authority with the Crown performing a dual function: head of the administrative apparatus and moderator of the political system. As moderator the monarch was the recipient of the political loyalty responsible for the stability of the system. The legal formula ascribed to the Crown the right to ignore or bypass regulations and customs whenever they conflicted with justice. The overall conception of justice was, of course, determined by factors not directly under the control of the monarch— social mores, religious beliefs, legal tradition, etc.—but the application of the general conception to specific cases was the royal prerogative. In accordance with the accepted cultural and legal principles, the Crown enjoyed supreme authority in the name of justice.

When early in 1541 *conquistador* Pedro de Valdivia

founded the city of Santiago, officially initiating in this manner the colonization of the country, he and his handful of soldiers brought with them the seeds of the political ideas and institutions that were going to determine the future of the colony.

The influence of those ideas and institutions on the life of colonial Chile was guaranteed by the attitude of the colonists. From their arrival in the new country, they showed a great desire to preserve their Spanish cultural identity. The existence of such a desire—which sometimes appears to have bordered on anxiety—is not difficult to understand. Peninsulars and creoles thought of the colony as an extension of Spain. Those born in the peninsula very logically considered themselves Spaniards while their children born in Chile were told from birth that they were also Spaniards. Discriminatory practices on the part of the government in Madrid did not present an insurmountable obstacle to the adoption of this line of thought by the latter group, especially since these discriminatory policies affected for a long time not only the creoles but other groups of peninsular-born as well. Finally, the great distance from Spain, plus the permanent Araucanian threat, tended to increase even more the colonists' need for a reaffirmation of their cultural identity.[1]

Such a deep concern with cultural identification was not conducive to the development of native forms. The creation of autochthonous institutions and ideas would have implied a direct threat to the preservation of Spanish culture in the colony. Therefore, original thinking was prevented and an imitative tendency became ingrained in Chilean colonial society.[2] Any attempt at independent

1. *Infra,* pp. 16f.
2. This development could, perhaps, also be explained in terms of the theory of cultural development stated in Louis Hartz, *op.*

self-assertion carried with it the implication that the colonists were not as Spanish as the inhabitants of the peninsula. Such admission was apparently unbearable. The only alternative was a loyalty to the Spanish forms that was founded on fear.

The reality of the colony did not fit the content of royal edicts and regulations. But neither did the reality in Spain fit the legal precepts under which it was supposedly regulated. Discrepancy between law and colonial reality did not interfere with the Chilean desire to be Spanish. On the contrary, it served as a reaffirmation of their coveted cultural identity. The idealistic precepts of colonial legislation were *accepted although not necessarily complied with*. Thus, institutional authoritism with its theoretical concern for justice and its dependence-based flexibility, became rooted in the colony.

In order to gain a closer view of how the system operated in Chile, it would be necessary to review its most important political institutions.

The Governor

The most prominent political figure of the colony was the governor. He was the representative of the king's executive power, the president of the *audiencia* (he was usually referred to as the "President") and the captain-general of the army.[3] According to the theoretical struc-

---

cit., p. 3: "For when a part of a European nation is detached from the whole of it, and hailed outward unto new soil, it loses the stimulus toward change that the whole provides. It lapses into a kind of immobility."

3. Due to the state of permanent war against the Araucanian Indians, a military establishment was kept in Chile. See Luis Galdames, *A History of Chile* (Chapel Hill: The University of North Carolina Press, 1941. Translated and edited by Isaac J. Cox), pp. 86ff.

ture of power provided for in the colonial legislation, the governor came under the direct supervision of the viceroy of Peru although, in practice, this subordination to Lima did not amount to much. His nominal dependence from this theoretically higher ranking official was superseded by the fact that he received his orders directly from Madrid.[4]

The geographic isolation of the colony, the almost permanent state of war against the Indians and, above all, the discretionary power with regard to the application or non-application of dispositions under the *se acata pero no se cumple* principle, added substantially to the political position of the governor. His power was indeed great although not total or absolute. He seems to have been the most important colonial official, but he was far from being the only wielder of political power in Chile.

The power of the governor was limited by the influence of other colonial forces. His control over the colony was checked by the Church authorities. He could not easily disregard the influence of those bishops with whom he often disagreed, but with whom he was also expected to maintain harmonious relations as representative of the Crown in the administration of the royal *patronato* over the Church. The governor also had to be careful in his dealings with the *audiencia,* the royal tribunal over which he presided without voting rights. To a lesser extent, he was required to court the good graces of the *cabildo.* Furthermore, his attributions and responsibilities were not clearly fixed, a situation which, in consonance with the Spanish political formula, forced

---

4. Leopoldo Castedo, *Resumen de la historia de Chile de Francisco Encina* (Santiago: Editorial Zig-Zag, S.A., 1954), Vol. I, pp. 253 and 258; see also, Dana G. Munro, *The Latin American Republics* (New York: D. Appleton-Century Co., Inc., 1942), p. 87.

upon him a certain degree of discretion in the use of his power. [5]

The Audiencia

During most of the colonial years, the *audiencia* of Santiago was the second most important political institution in the colony.[6] The *audiencia* had the double function of a court of justice and a political body. As a judicial institution it was the highest court of appeals in the colony. As a political organism it supervised the governor by reporting to Madrid on his public performance and personal conduct, and was empowered to name a temporary successor should he die in office.[7] The members of the audiencia were royal appointees called *oidores*. They were expected, together with their duties as members of the judiciary, to "report to the king about all matters pertaining to the government of the colony."[8]

The decisions of the *audiencia* did not, however, bind the governor and when a conflict arose between the two, the governor's ruling would usually prevail.[9] In the meantime, the *audiencia* could try, if it was sufficiently

5. Luis Galdames, *Historia de Chile: la evolución constitucional* (Santiago: Bacells y Cía., 1925), Vol. p. 48.
6. The royal *audiencia* of Chile was first established in Concepción from August 1567 to June 1575, then in Santiago from September 1609 to April 1811, and once more during the Spanish reconquest of that town from 1814–1817. On this subject see Francisco Frías Valenzuela, *Historia de Chile* (Santiago: Editorial Nascimento, 1947), Vol. I, p. 307; and Francisco A. Encina, *Historia de Chile* (Third Edition; Santiago: Editorial Nascimento, 1950), Vol. II, pp. 5ff.
7. *Catálogo del Archivo de la Real Audiencia de Santiago*, published by the Biblioteca Nacional de Chile (Santiago: Imprenta, Litografía y Encuadernación Barcelona, 1898), pp. Vff.
8. Castedo, *op. cit.*, Vol. I, p. 255.
9. Encina, *op. cit.*, Vol. III, pp. 494ff.

interested in the issue in question, to win the Crown over to its point of view.[10] While the governor commanded explicit executive powers in his capacity as captain-general and direct representative of the monarchy, the *oidores'* supervisory function could only prevail in the colony through the permissiveness of a weak governor or by an overt expression of royal support.

The power of the *audiencia*, then, depended on the ability of the *oidores* to influence the actions of the governor or to gain the royal ear. When disagreement between the colonial executive and the *audiencia* flared up, the *oidores* would turn to the king for help. Royal support, if secured, would take the form of a favorable edict or would result in the appointment of a new governor.

A favorable royal resolution was a proof of the *oidores'* influence at the court, that could, under propitious circumstances, tilt the colonial balance of power in their favor. After all, the future of the governor was in the hands of the monarch. The king could not only dismiss the governor at will but he could also influence the results of the special process of investigation (*residencia*) colonial officials underwent at the end of their terms in office, and he could send a special judge (*visitador*) to conduct an on-the-spot investigation.

The Cabildo

The third center of political power in colonial Chile resided in the *cabildo* or municipal council.[11] The *cabildo* was the representative body of the *vecinos* (neighbors)

---

10. *Catálogo...*, *op. cit.*, pp. Vff.
11. Much has been said and written about this colonial institution and its character and nature have been widely discussed. For a sound description of it see Zorraquín, *op. cit.*, pp. 64.

with *casa poblada* (inhabited house). The right to be a member of the *cabildo* was enjoyed only by a minority of the population, which was in fact its leading class. Those who had been entrusted with *encomiendas* (Indians) were the original *vecinos,* but later on membership in the *cabildo* was opened to the heads of families rooted in the city. Royal functionaries were usually excluded from membership. Likewise excluded were almost all Indians, *mestizos,* and freemen of the country. While the offices of governor and *oidores* were filled by peninsular Spaniards with no roots in the colony, the seats in the *cabildo* were occupied by members of the most distinguished creole families, who represented the ideas and interests of the landed aristocracy.[12]

There were several *cabildos* in colonial Chile although it could safely be stated that only the *cabildo* of Santiago and to a lesser extent that of Concepción wielded any considerable degree of power.[13] Their main function was to serve as a bridge between the governor and the population at large. Every time a new order was promulgated, the governor would inform the *cabildo.* Its members would inform the *vecinos* who in turn—only if necessary, of course—would inform the rest of the population. Communications passed both downward and upward. The

12. Jaime Eyzaguirre, *Fisonomía histórica de Chile* (México City: Fondo de Cultura Económica, 1948), pp. 56ff. Julio Alemparte, *El cabildo en Chile colonial* (Santiago: Ediciones de la Universidad de Chile, 1940), pp. 16f.; Néstor Meza Villalobos, *La conciencia política chilena durante la monarquía* (Santiago: Editorial Universitaria, S.A., 1958), pp. 57f. and pp. 71ff.; and Haring, *op. cit.,* pp. 175f.

13. In this work, when mentioning the *cabildo,* I will be referring to that of Santiago. A more detailed analysis of the political life of the colony would require the treatment of the *cabildo* of Concepción as a separate political entity.

feelings and opinions of the *vecinos* frequently reached the governor and the *audiencia* through the *cabildo*.

The *cabildo* of Santiago, founded by conqueror de Valdivia himself, was to be found from the time of its early life, fully engaged in the colonial power struggle. As the representative of the creoles, the *cabildo* was in constant friction with the other colonial institutions, especially with the *audiencia* that was the usual representative of the peninsular interests and population.

At the beginning of the colonization, the *cabildo* had been a rather powerful entity in Chile, but the establishment of the royal *audiencia* meant a decrease in its powers.[14] Not only was the *audiencia* vested with a higher official rank than the *cabildo*, but it eventually took away some of the political functions which had been performed by the municipal organ.[15]

The *cabildo* was the institutional device that permitted direct contact between the creole aristocracy and the monarch. Like the other colonial organs of government, the *cabildo* was able to communicate directly with the Crown. In a disagreement with the other colonial forces, or with the laws of the Crown, the *cabildo* would appeal directly to the monarch.[16] In their pleas to the king, the municipal officials would usually emphasize their noble ancestry and the deeds and sacrifices their forefathers had performed for the Crown.[17]

By having easy access to the Crown, the municipal body was able to exercise some check upon the other colonial institutions in more or less the same manner as

---

14. Meza. *op. cit.,* pp. 57f.
15. Eyzaguirre., *op. cit.,* p. 63.
16. Meza, *op. cit.,* p. 37.
17. *Ibid.,* pp. 48ff.

described in the case of the *audiencia*. The members of the *cabildo* wrote and sent delegates to Madrid to promote their opinions and defend their interests. This opportunity provided the creole aristocracy with an outlet for complaints and frustrations that instead of threatening the system increased dependence on the monarch. Therefore, when the *cabildo* developed ill feelings, they were directed not toward the king in Madrid, but against the other colonial institutions with which it was competing for hegemony. The *se acata pero no se cumple* principle vested upon the governor responsibility for the enforcement or non-enforcement of the royal edicts. If his decision was opposed by the *cabildo*, he, the governor, would be the recipient of its enmity. The *cabildo*'s hostility was, of course, extended as well to any other official or institution with which it may have found itself at loggerheads. In the midst of the continuous colonial conflict for power, and in disregard of the official hierarchical structure, the *cabildo* "functioned in practice as an independent entity within the monarchical authority."[18]

The Church

The Catholic Church in colonial Chile constituted a definite center of political power.[19] The evangelic zeal of the conquest and the Catholic character of the monarchy placed the religious institutions in a position of influence. From the beginnings of the colonial period on, frequent complaints were heard about the political activities of the Church. In 1583 Alonso de Sotomayor wrote to the king: "The bishops, provincials and delegates of the Holy

---

18. Alemparte, *op. cit.*, pp. 117f.
19. Diego Barros Arana, *Historia general de Chile* (Second Edition; Santiago: Editorial Nascimento, 1932-1933), Vol. III, p. 152.

Office have come to have so much authority that the one who governs has no choice but to do as they wish."[20]

During all the years that Chile was under colonial rule, the different religious orders and ecclesiastical authorities actively participated in political affairs. This participation was not limited to the high ranking Church officials. Almost every priest and clergyman seem to have had enough time and energy to persistently attack the governor or any other colonial institution, and to propose all kinds of political projects to the viceroy and the monarch.[21]

The case of Father Luis de Valdivia of the Jesuit order, who after long pleas to the king was entrusted with the direction of the war against the Araucanians, is just one example of the direct participation of the Church in the political life of the colony.[22] The famous conflict which took place between Governor Francisco de Meneses and the bishop of Santiago[23] is another illustration of the political involvement of the Church.[24]

20. As quoted in Encina, *op. cit.,* Vol. II, p. 262.

21. *Ibid.,* Vol. II, p. 265.

22. For an account of the personality and political activities of Father Valdivia see Encina, *op. cit.,* Vol. III, pp. 78ff.; and Crescente Errázuriz, *Historia de Chile durante los gobiernos de García Ramón, Merlo de la Fuente y Jaraquemada* (Santiago: Imprenta Cervantes, 1908), Vol. II, Chapter XXV.

23. Encina, *op. cit.,* Vol. III, Chapter XIV, describes the fight between Governor Meneses and Bishop Humanzoro. On the same subject see Domingo Amunátegui y Solar, *Historia de Chile: la dominación española* (Santiago: Bacells y Cía., 1925), pp. 156ff. For a description of the conflict between Governor Alonso de la Ribera and Bishop Juan Pérez de Espinoza see Amunátegui, *ibid.,* pp. 92f. and pp. 244f.

24. Frías, *op. cit.,* Vol. I, pp. 352f., believes that the religious orders were actually more powerful than the bishops. He bases this assertion on the fact that the bishop of Santiago was frequently unfamiliar with the environment and always encountered hostility on the part of the regular clergy. For these rea-

Some governors found it necessary to write letters to the monarch complaining about clergymen's interference in political matters.[25] It is also quite probable that the political influence of the Church did not achieve higher peaks because of the internal rivalries that consumed so much of the time and energy of the regular and secular priests and of the monastic orders. Conflicts between the different religious groups and ecclesiastical authorities were quite frequent and constituted one of the most colorful characteristics of colonial life.[26] The monastic orders, the regular clergy, and the secular priests not only fought each other with zeal and dedication, but each group was also beset with internal conflicts.

In its quest for political power, the Church found a useful tool in its spiritual ascendancy over the population of the colony, especially in its power to excommunicate.[27] But in any final analysis, the real basis for the Church's political influence can be found in its links to the Crown. In the colony the Church acted as an official branch of the royal administration. Through an agreement with the Vatican, the colonial Church was placed under the direct control of the Spanish king. The Church was, in practice, part of the official governing apparatus. Lacking wide independent basis of power, it was ultimately

sons Frías thinks the bishop was less influential in social and political matters than the religious orders.

25. Castedo, *op. cit.,* Vol. I, pp. 240f.

26. The disputes between the religious orders and the authorities often took violent form. For a description of some of these heated episodes see Encina, *op. cit.,* Vol. II, pp. 164ff.; and Castedo, *op. cit.,* Vol. I, p. 245.

27. As an illustration of how the religious authorities used their power to excommunicate for non-religious purposes see the account of the fight between the bishop of Santiago and Captain Huerta over the testament of Sánchez in Errázuriz, *op. cit.,* Vol. II, Chapter XVII.

through royal sanction that the Church could fulfill its political aspirations. The members of the Church were, thus, among the most assiduous writers to the monarch. Their correspondence with the Crown covered a great variety of topics—from complaints against the governor to attacks on the rival religious orders and ecclesiastical dignitaries. As Francisco Encina has asserted, it seems as if "the activity of the clergy was directed, preferably, to the task of writing communications and letters to the king."[28]

The Crown

The hierarchical structure so carefully designed by the colonial laws of Spain was in effect only the superficial layer of an authoritistic system that allowed a high degree of political interplay among the colonial institutions. It was through their relationship to the Crown that colonial institutions and groups derived political influence and legitimized their power. There were potentially independent sources of power, but, within the accepted political culture, royal sanction was the legitimizing agent— the Crown elicited the allegiance that made authority possible.[29]

The certain degree of initiative and independence manifested by the different colonial political units was the result of the direct connection existing between the Crown and the different colonial institutions. The king

---

28. Encina, *op. cit.*, Vol. II, p. 262, explains that the writing of letters to the king was by no means limited to the members of the Church. As he said, "Every person who was able to handle a pen thought himself under the obligation to follow the example of the clergy."
29. On the relationship between authority and legitimacy see Lasswell and Kaplan, *op. cit.*, p. 134.

was looked upon as the only source of legitimacy. For the colonists, accepted and legitimate power was, in practical terms, the ability to elicit royal support or consent. In colonial Chile the king was the unchallenged symbol of supreme authority and the center around which the political life of the Colony took place.[30]

The king of Spain acted as final judge on any dispute that arose among the colonial organs of government. In this way he was able to preserve loyalty to the mother country on the part of the colonists.[31] All complaints and petitions would be addressed to the Crown in constant reassertion of the authoritistic equation.

The Chilean historian Diego Barros Arana, in analyzing the relationship between the Crown and the colonial institutions, arrived at the conclusion that the system was designed with the conscious intention of providing for constant reciprocal supervision among the different colonial forces.[32] But whether purposely organized or just the result of an involuntary process, the system of reciprocal and constant checks, based on the acceptance of absolute royal supremacy, preserved the colonial dependency on Madrid.[33]

Struggle for Power

In Chile, allegiance to the Crown was consolidated through local friction. So widespread and firmly entrenched was the conflict among the different colonial

---

30. Meza, *op. cit.,* p. 19.
31. Jaime Eyzaguirre, *Ideario y ruta de la emancipación chilena* (Santiago: Editorial Universitaria, S. A., 1957), p. 26.
32. Barros, *op. cit.,* Vol. VIII, p. 353.
33. On the royal control of the colonial bureaucracy see Charles E. Chapman, *A History of Spain* (New York: The Macmillan Co., 1918), pp. 287f. and Ots, *op. cit.,* pp. 49ff.

officials and institutions, that Benjamín Vicuña Mackenna describes the history of the colony as follows: "Civil history: fight between the bishops and the Presidents (Governors); judicial history: fight between the *audiencia* and everybody else."[34]

The executive attributions were vested on the governor who could choose to enforce the laws and regulations enacted in Madrid. If the other centers of colonial power were in disagreement with the governor's decision, as was very often the case, they had institutional means at their disposal with which to defy him. Letters and representatives would be sent to Madrid with detailed expositions of the reasons why the governor's decision—or the royal order itself—was opposed. While these appeals, usually presented by the *audiencia,* the *cabildo,* or the Church, would run their course, the rule of the governor would tend to prevail, but his actions were constantly subject to scrutiny by the complaints of the colonists and the revisions of the Crown.

The governor was not the only one whose power was constantly under the threat of royal revocation. The actions of the *cabildo,* the behavior of the *audiencia,* and the conduct of the Church were all under the same danger. And the more they opposed each other, the easier it became to preserve this state of affairs.[35]

The constant friction and competition were clearly reflected in the colonial correspondence with the Crown. All colonial quarrels were dutifully communicated to Madrid where it was hoped that the monarch would find

34. *Historia crítica y social de la ciudad de Santiago* (Santiago: Imprenta de Prisiones, 1938).
35. For an analysis of another situation in which checks among dependent units tended to increase dependence from a central organ see Frank, *op. cit.,* pp. 8ff.

a solution.[36] The apparent flexibility present in the colonial system was the logical by-product of authoritism. Dependence upon a monistic center of legitimacy paved the way for rivalry between the dependent units. As a result of the Crown's philosophical and juridical commitment to justice, the monarch was expected to listen to everyone. Such royal availability worked toward a real reduction of formal hierarchical distinctions between colonial institutions and tended to encourage political competition among them.

Moderating Power

As stated before, the Spanish Crown performed two main functions: head of the administrative apparatus and moderator of the system. It was the convergence of these two roles on the monarch that gave the system its authoritistic character. As the head of the administration the king had power, and through his moderating faculties such power was legitimized.

> The will of the monarch circulated through the colonial structure not as the result of inflexible despotism, but with a rare and prudent ductility. The spirit of the race had made the king a *moderating power*.[37]

The traditional Roman-Spanish conception of the monarch as the seeker of justice and the achiever of the common good assigned him a position above the law and carried with it the idealization of the Crown. The

---

36. As far as I know, there is no available analysis of the colony's correspondence with the king. Such a study could prove of great value in determining the actual behavior of the colonial institutions.

37. Eyzaguirre, *Fisonomía...*, *op. cit.*, pp. 56f. (Italics mine).

king was looked upon in Chile as the all-powerful figure who had been entrusted by God with the welfare of his subjects.[38] The great distance from Spain, if anything, helped in furthering this process of idealization.[39] So accepted was the idealized image of the monarch, that José Antonio Rojas wrote of the Chileans almost at the end of the colonial period: ". . . they believe in the king as they believe in God."[40]

Psychologically, the idealization of the king was intimately related to his moderating capacity. His functions in this role were easily distinguishable. It was as the God-appointed guardian and leader of the nation that the monarch of Spain became, in the name of justice, the equivalent of an ultimate court of appeals. Within the cultural system in which he was operating, the monarch acted as supreme political and judicial organ.

This combination of political and judicial supremacy underlaid the colonial life of Chile. The direct and constant connection between the Crown in its moderating capacity and the colonists was both a result of the Spanish conception of authority and an active agent in its preservation. It would be extremely difficult to determine exactly to what degree the relations between colonial institutions and Crown were the product of a phenomenon which had been developed primarily in the peninsula, and to what extent colonial circumstances contributed to its continuation and success. The best we can do is to realize the broad cultural implications involved in the existence of such an attitude toward the monarch. The Chilean colonial mind was willing to accept the

38. Alemparte, *op. cit.,* p. 95.
39. Sergio Villalobos, *Tradición y reforma en 1810* (Santiago: Ediciones de la Universidad de Chile, 1961), p. 73.
40. As quoted by Eyzaguirre, *Fisonomía. . . , op. cit.,* pp. 83f.

authoritistic implications that went along with the moderating functions of the Crown. The result was a colonial allegiance to the Crown which, translated into broader political terms, meant loyalty to Spain.[41]

One of the most significant aspects of the relationship between the Crown and its subjects was a certain inability, on the part of the subjects, to deal effectively with their own problems. Dependence on the Crown and continuous internal strife precluded collective cooperation among those affected. Whenever a problematic situation developed, or a political task had to be performed, the colonists did not feel culturally obliged or institutionally compelled to act upon it themselves. The feelings of an articulate community were absent. The sense of collective responsibility did not develop. The answer to all political problems was to refer them to the monarch who had the power and the duty to redress their grievances and find solution to their problems. Lack of collective responsibility became one of the basic psycho-political characteristics of the system and it was one of the forces that allowed it to operate successfully.

The certain degree of local initiative present in colonial Chile had a negative or suspensive character. The colonial officials were legally entitled to disagree with the royal solutions and dispositions, but they were precluded

---

41. There are indications that this loyalty began to falter under Bourbon rule. The policies of the new dynasty, especially under Carlos III, tended to alter the relationships upon which authoritism rested. It is interesting to realize that under the Bourbons the need for a military establishment in the colonies was strongly felt in Madrid. This emergence of militarism could be interpreted as an attempt to replace decreasing allegiance with the threat of violence. Such an interpretation could provide the basis for useful hypotheses concerning the role of the military.

from initiating any positive action of their own. They could only request and complain—the two alternatives that a despotic father would usually allow his children.

The moderating role of the Crown has to be analyzed in relation to the political psychology of the colonists. Only in this light can we understand why the system functioned for almost three hundred years without facing any serious crises or challenges. The royal image provided a symbol of authority that was culturally acceptable to the inhabitants of Chile.[42] Furthermore, the king's willingness to listen to the colonists and the constant local strife provided escape for the passions, antagonistic feelings, and frictions which might have, otherwise, found very different political expression.

Internally, direct universal links with the monarch made it impossible for any one institution or person to achieve total control. The governors of Chile, due to their executive responsibilities, were in a better position than anyone else to become the undisputed rulers of the colony. Some of them tried to do just that, and a few succeeded for a short while. Eventually, however, the slow but effective process of checking and counterchecking began to take effect. Appeals and complaints would go to the Crown, and through the Crown the internal balance of forces would be reestablished.[43] As long as the colonists accepted the king as final judge and protector, their loyalty to the system was guaranteed. The moderating function of the monarch—with all the complex of cul-

---

42. It would probably be quite rewarding to interpret the role of the Spanish monarch in terms of Sebastian de Grazia's theories of leadership. Such an effort would contribute to the broadening of our findings by providing meaningful and provocative bases for comparative analysis.

43. See the abuses of authority committed by Governor Meneses and the responses to them in Amunátegui, *op. cit.,* Chapter XIII.

tural, political and psychological factors that it involved—symbolized the stability of Spanish colonial rule.

Authoritism in Chile

The dependence of colonial Chile on the monarchy cannot be explained, of course, in political terms alone. The political organization of the colony responded to—or at least was in accord with—anthropological tendencies of a marked nature. The existence of the authoritistic relationship between the monarch and his subjects is most suggestive of similar patterns of social and psychological behavior. The whole complex of personal interrelations characteristic of the cultural entity was permeated with the same inclination that was so markedly present in its political organization.

The acceptance of the royal monopoly of authority, as symbolized in the colonial idealization of the king, diverted any actual criticism of existing conditions from reaching His Catholic Majesty. Whatever went wrong in the administration of the colony was taken to be the fault of the colonial officials. The king was never to be blamed. His ministers, delegates, and representatives were responsible for any failure or mistake.[44] In the words of Jaime Eyzaguirre, "an absolute separation took place in the creole mind between the monarch and his bad representatives in America."[45] This colonial attitude created, in practice, a situation in which the possessor of final authority was not held responsible to the community for its use. Theoretically, the monarch was responsible to God and his conscience for his performance as a ruler. In practice, however, he did not have to account to anyone

---

44. Villalobos, *op. cit.*, p. 73.
45. Eyzaguirre, *Fisonomía. . . , op. cit.*, p. 85.

for his actions. This interpretation of political responsibility has remained one of the most deeply rooted characteristics of the Spanish-American people.

The political life of colonial Chile was organized around the governor, the *audiencia,* the *cabildo,* and the Church. The balance of power among these four institutions was not static but rather fluid. The governors had the upper hand most of the time due to their executive capacity but factors such as personal character, the integrity of the *oidores,* the prestige of the bishops, and the military situation in the fight against the Indians, frequently introduced changes in the colonial balance of power. This interplay of forces was the real political structure, and it had been made possible and operational by the acceptance of the king as the final judge in all disputes. Furthermore, the power of the colonial officials was related to their ability to influence royal action. As a result these institutions developed a vested interest in preserving the relationship which legitimized their own power. It is no wonder that in almost three centuries of Spanish domination, Chile never seriously challenged the colonial system.

III.

The Breakdown of the Colonial System

Controversy over the real nature of the emancipation movement in the Spanish American colonies has been long and heated. Hypothetical causes most commonly advanced to justify the emancipation have been the antagonism between creoles and peninsulars, the discrimination practiced against the native-born in the distribution of public offices, the economic policies of Spain, and the influence of the American and French revolutions.[1] There can be little doubt that these four factors were all present as active elements in the life of colonial Chile. Nevertheless, to ascribe to one or any combination of them, ultimate responsibility for the colony's independence would be most unwarranted.

Antagonism between American-born and Spanish-born colonists prevailed from the beginning. For hundreds of years an active, militant hostility existed between

---

1. The anti-Spanish activities of the Jews, Jesuits, and Freemasons have also been cited as causes of the independence movement. See de Madariaga, *op. cit.,* Vol. II, pp. 264ff.

different regional groups; the fights between Andalusians, Castilians, Basques, Asturians, creoles and the rest were fixed features of colonial life.[2] In later colonial history there had been a polarization of forces, and a general identification along creole and peninsular lines replaced the previous multiple groupings; but this polarization did not alter the basic fact that the regional conflict was well under political control.

The fights between regional groups were prevented from acquiring dangerous political overtones not because of the application of physical coercion by Spain, but because of the system of institutional authoritism. The system permitted a certain degree of internal flexibility among regional groups as well as among colonial political institutions. But the acknowledgement by all parties of the Crown's authority in its moderating capacity meant that ultimately whatever flexibility there was, was rooted in the acceptance of royal legal and moral supremacy. Even immediately prior to the break from Spain, there is little evidence that the colonial system might have developed malfunctions serious enough to challenge royal control or the allegiance paid to it.

The theory that secession from Spain was prompted by a creole desire for a greater share of public office has also been frequently overplayed.[3] The desire to control

2. de Madariaga, "El auge del imperio español en América," in *op. cit.*, Vol. II, pp. 32 and 37.

3. "The roots of the war of independence are not looked for any longer—as was the case during the last century—in a series of 'complaints' or 'claims' of the kingdom of Chile against Spain. This understanding of the 'causes of the independence' elaborated by Barros Arana and Luis Galdames, and which our school textbooks have made so popular, is not recognized as valid today. This interpretation resulted from an imperfect knowledge of the facts involved and furthermore, was heavily influenced by the passions that emerged during the war of

more public positions did, of course, exist on the part of the native-born. Nevertheless, as with the previous problem, the existence of an area of friction cannot properly explain the events leading up to independence. The important question that has to be answered to justify this hypothesis is why this problem suddenly acquired political relevancy after having been under effective check for so many years.

The attempt to explain the loss of the colonies in terms of Spanish economic exploitation has generally been the result of the modern emphasis on economic relationships and does not appear to be any better founded historically than the former interpretations. Furthermore, the acceptance of this hypothesis would lead to logical conclusions that might well be in contradiction with its implicit premises. The economic policies of Spain were greatly liberalized under the Bourbon dynasty. If this liberalization brought discontent to the colonies, it would have done so either because the colonies favored conservative measures or because they expected a much greater degree of liberalization. Had the latter been true, it would be necessary to explain how partial satisfaction of the colonists' desires, rather than having a placating effect, encouraged them to take as drastic a step as independence. If the former is accepted, the proponents of the economic explanation would, in effect, be asserting that the colonists revolted because the economic principles of the new dynasty were far too liberal for their taste. Discontent with Spanish economic policies did probably exist in creole circles. But that this dissatisfaction provoked the break

independence, as well as by an anti-Spanish prejudice derived from religious sectarism." Gonzalo Vial Correa, *La nueva bibliografía sobre las causas de la independencia de Chile* (Santiago: Editorial Universidad Católica, 1961), p. 3.

from Spain is most difficult to substantiate historically since all indications are that the colonists had been quite pleased by the commercial policies of Bourbon enlightened despotism.

To attribute responsibility for the early nineteenth century emancipation in the Spanish colonies to the American and French revolutions is also highly questionable. While the influence of the revolutions was obviously felt by the individual colonists, the French and American experience cannot be cited as an immediate cause of independence. Once the new republics were established, however, French and American ideas gained importance. When those in power sought new political formulas to justify their rule, American and French forms as well as British examples served as alternatives to the Spanish authoritistic devices.

Often the attempts to account for independence on these ideological grounds have evolved from a desire to find similarities between American and Latin American emancipation movements. Historical evidence reveals the contrary, however, and compels agreement with William W. Sweet's judgement: "The causes of the South American wars for independence were far different from those which resulted in the rebellion of England's thirteen colonies. . . ."[4] The tendency of many American analysts to explain the breaking away of the Spanish colonies in terms of a projection of the American colonial experience is understandable and justifiable, but it results in a lack of awareness about the real character of the colonial split from Spanish rule.

In Chile the forces that were to run rampant after the collapse of Spanish control had been present in the

4. *A History of Latin America* (New York: The Abingdon Press, n.d.), p. 157.

country long before the nineteenth century. It had been the ultimate adherence of the colonists to the system of authoritistic royal control that had kept them from exploding into deadly political controversies.

> It would appear astonishing that so many years had gone by without there having erupted the fight that had been brewing for so long. Nevertheless, it is necessary to take into consideration one of the influences that predominated in the colonial society. That influence was the religious veneration that was paid to the sovereign. Regardless of the number of offenses, the profound acceptance of the authority of the monarch silenced, or weakened, the most justified complaints.[5]

If Spanish authoritism was the force that maintained a balance in the colony, and if submission to the monarch kept the antagonistic regional feelings, the competing economic and institutional interests, and all other possible anarchical tendencies in check, then any valuable interpretation of the instability that plagued the nation during the early years of the nineteenth century must begin by explaining what happened to the system that had for so long preserved loyalty to Spain.

The Downfall of the Spanish Crown

The independence of Chile is closely related to the breakdown of royal authority that took place with the Napoleonic invasion of Spain. The importance of this as the factor directly responsible for the independence of the colony is better appreciated when the general political situation of the country, immediately prior to 1808, is taken into account.

5. Miguel Luis Amunátegui, *La crónica de 1810* (Santiago: Imprenta de la República de Jacinto Núñez, 1876), Vol. I, p. 119.

At the beginning of the nineteenth century Chileans showed no appreciable signs of being interested in changing their political dependency. Referring to this absence of any widespread desire for a break, Miguel Luis Amunátegui has stated: ". . . in the first months of 1808 the great majority—I could almost say the unanimity—of Chileans were sincerely and profoundly devoted to the monarch and the metropolis."[6] Some individuals and even some small groups did harbor the idea of independence.[7] If Napoleon had not invaded Spain when he did, this small pro-independence minority might have in due time, and in combination with other factors, provoked the separation from Spain. In the years prior to Napoleon's take-over, however, the scattered forces did not present any serious challenge to Spanish colonial rule.

> It is undeniable that at that time there were already some creoles who had something more in mind than merely desires for a reform, and that they went as far as to wish for a revolutionary break with Spain. But the truth is that they were very few and that these ideas did not flourish spontaneously in their own land . . . it is very difficult to imagine that they would have gone any further without the unforeseen and favorable occasion which the Napoleonic invasion of Spain presented.[8]

Under these circumstances it is difficult to estimate how long Spanish rule might have lasted had the events in Europe taken a different course.

On March 19, 1808, Carlos IV, King of Spain, abdi-

---

6. *Ibid.,* p. 169.
7. This lack of desire to break away from Spain was probably not upset by the Bourbon rulers to any appreciable degree. An improvement in the quality of the administration under this dynasty is generally accepted by Chilean historians.
8. Eyzaguirre, *Fisonomia . . . , op. cit.,* pp. 84f.

cated his Crown in favor of his son who then became the new monarch under the name of Fernando VII. Napoleon, whose troops were in the process of taking over Spain, forced Fernando to return the crown to his father. Carlos was then forced to give it to Napoleon in the treaty of May 5, 1808, with the condition that he preserve the integrity and independence of the country under the rule of a prince of his own choosing.[9] That prince was Napoleon's brother, Joseph, King of Holland. Opposition to the new monarch quickly developed and the majority of the Spaniards, still considering Fernando their rightful king, began to battle for his return.[10]

Local juntas were rapidly established in the capitals of the provinces, each one proclaiming its right to rule until the rightful monarch was returned to power.[11] A *Junta Central* was set up as the supreme organism to which local juntas were to send their delegates. The deterioration of the military situation prompted its move from Aranjuez to Seville, and then to Cadiz where it named a Regency of five men entrusted with the responsibilities of government and of convening the *Cortes* or Spanish parliament. The local juntas, the *Junta Central*, the Regency, and later the *Cortes* all claimed to be acting as the rightful government of the country until Fernando could repossess his throne. They did not challenge the

---

9. The treaty also provided for the preservation of Catholicism as the official religion of the country. Rafael Altamira y Crevea, *Manual de historia de España* (Second Edition; Buenos Aires: Editorial Sudamericana, 1946), pp. 462ff.; and Antonio Ballesteros y Beretta, *Historia de España y su influencia en la historia universal* (Barcelona: Salvat Editores, S.A., 1934), Vol. VII, pp. 5ff.

10. Altamira, *op. cit.*, pp. 464f.; and Ballesteros, *op. cit.*, Vol. VII, pp. 17ff.

11. Altamira, *op. cit.*, p. 472; and Ballesteros, *op. cit.*, Vol. VII, pp. 35ff.

power of the monarch, but declared themselves the temporary depositories of the king's right to rule.[12] From 1808 to 1814, Spain was practically without a ruler since Fernando was imprisoned by Napoleon, and Joseph Bonaparte was never able to exercise full control over the country. The government of the Spanish American colonies came to depend upon the *Junta*, Regency, and *Cortes* that formed the anti-Napoleonic machinery. These different institutions enjoyed, however, only a most precarious power due to the country's entanglement in civic and international conflicts whose consequences were unforeseeable.[13]

The sudden removal of the king from his throne altered the colonial arrangement. The traditionally accepted mechanism for resolving disputes and preserving order no longer operated and its replacement, the Spanish *Junta*, was doomed to failure. It proved unable to assume the moderating power of the monarch or to substitute, in an acceptable way, for the complex variety of administrative functions the Crown had played in three hundred years of colonial life. Nor could the new institution replace the powerful symbol of the Crown in the colonial mind. The king of Spain was more than a mere political instrument that could be replaced by any other political institution. He was the sociopsychological force that kept Spanish colonial authoritism in working order. When Napoleon overthrew the monarchy, he not only broke the link between Spain and the colonies, he also cut the tie that united the colonial institutions themselves.

---

12. Chapman, *op. cit.*, pp. 492f.
13. For a description of these events see Ballesteros, *op. cit.*, Vol. VII, pp. 30ff. Fernando VII did not return to the Spanish throne until March 22, 1814, but his return did not end the internal struggle. For an account of the rule of Fernando see Ballesteros, *op. cit.*, Vol. VII, pp. 135ff.

News of the events in Europe arrived slowly in Chile. Initially loyalty to Fernando was not questioned, of course, but different interpretations of what should be done until he could assume power did emerge.[14] The creoles, realizing the vast opportunities presented by the new situation, designed a solution aimed at gaining supremacy over their traditional colonial enemies—the governor, the *audiencia,* and the Church. In order to take power in their own hands, they campaigned for the creation of a local junta. They maintained that, as had already been done in Spain, a local junta should govern until Fernando's return, and substantiated their position by claiming that it was the only one in accordance with the contractual basis of the Spanish monarchy.[15] Specifically, they argued that the imprisonment of the king and the obedience paid by the Council of Castile to the Napoleonic orders had ultimately broken the laws of succession and remitted to the nation the right to constitute a new government. According to the contractual origin of political power and the equality of the various kingdoms united to Spain through the monarch, none of them could assume the right to form a government or expect obedience without first being recognized as legitimate by the rest. Thus, it was not essential to accept and to obey the *Junta* of Seville; it was enough to swear allegiance to Fernando VII.[16]

---

14. Villalobos, *op. cit.,* p. 161.
15. The contractual interpretation of the origin of government was built on the assumption that God had given absolute power to the king *through the people,* and it found ample expression in the writings of St. Isidore, Vitoria, and Suárez among other Spanish writers. This contractual theory had been claimed by the local juntas in Spain as the basis for their power.
16. Néstor Meza Villalobos, *La actividad política del reino de Chile entre 1806 y 1810* (Santiago: Editorial Universitaria, S.A., 1946), p. 42.

To properly understand the colonial reaction to these events, it must be kept in mind that the authoritistic arrangement was not necessarily consciously understood by those who had worked under it for so long. The actual allocation of authority and power had been rationalized in terms not necessarily consistent with the actual nature and functional characteristics of the system. Once the functional characteristics were drastically altered by the sudden removal of the Crown, the accepted rationalizations, as well as the reality of the internal political strife in the colony, came to the forefront.

While the creoles who possessed many potential instruments of power favored radical change in the colonial structure, the Spanish officials, mostly peninsulars with no basis of power other than their link with the mother country, preferred no changes. Their point of view was expressed in a pamphlet supposedly written by a Spanish clerk named Ignacio Torres. Its title provides a good description of its contents: "Warning to the people of Chile, calling them to preserve their loyalty in the defense of the religion, the king, and the fatherland, without listening to the seditionists who suggest revolutionary ideas in view of the latest developments in Spain."[17] They advocated the temporary replacement of the Crown by the *Junta* of Seville at the apex of the colonial system and justified their stand by accepting the *Junta's* claim that it was the legal substitute for the deposed monarch.[18] It was of prime importance for the peninsular officials to elicit acceptance of the government in Spain if they were to retain their power and influence in the colony.

---

17. The full text of this document is reproduced in M.L. Amunátegui, *op. cit.,* pp. 184ff.
18. Meza, *La actividad . . . , op. cit.,* p. 139.

Prolongation of the European conflict sharpened the differences among the colonists. Without the controlling royal influence, the struggle between the creoles and the peninsulars was no longer aimed at specific political objectives but at the total domination of the country. They were not interested in concrete concessions from one another, but rather each group sought total elimination of the other from the political scene. Such a conception of power was perfectly in tune with their traditional monistic and absolutistic interpretation of political authority and organization.

The desire to subdue all opposing colonial institutions emanated from the political culture of the colony and it rested on the idea of complete control, not on shared authority or coordinate jurisdiction. In the colonial political psyche and cultural tradition, total power was the only kind worth seeking. The Crown had restrained these conflicting forces not by creating a compromising capacity but by channeling their absolutistic inclinations through an authoritistic system of government. Adherence to authoritism had been assured by the implicit possibility that any group could obtain total control by influencing the king's will. A contemporary Chilean historian, analyzing creole dissatisfaction with the distribution of public offices during colonial days describes this concept of power: ". . . the creoles did not aspire to control the majority of the public positions; they aspired to monopolize them."[19]

The creole quest for power did not originally imply separatist intentions. The obstacles in their way were their traditional enemies—the other colonial centers of power. It would be highly simplistic to believe that expressions

_____

19. Vial, *op. cit.*, p. 7.

of loyalty to Fernando were, at this point, false. There were no practical reasons for the creole aristocracy to object to their traditional allegiance to the monarch. Furthermore, now that the king was a symbol of legitimacy lacking any actual power, it would have been inconceivable for the creoles to forfeit the obvious political benefits of claiming loyalty while trying to eliminate their enemies. Néstor Meza argues that at this point in Chilean history, the creole "claim of love for the monarchy and for the king was sincere and made in good faith."[20] In Chile, as in the rest of the colonies, the first actions of what was to become a movement for independence were not aimed against the king or against the mother country; rather they were directed against the Spanish officials in the colony.[21]

The break of the colony with Spain was actually the result of a process that started when the first news of the Napoleonic coup reached Chile. Events slowly evolved into a clearly defined movement for independence. The emancipation idea seems to have been an outcome, not a cause of this process.[22] Once the Crown was removed, the unifying link ceased to exist and the empire began to disintegrate. Institutionally and psychologically, the *Junta Central,* the Regency, and the *Cortes* could neither command the loyalty rendered to the Crown nor replace it even temporarily. The political stability of

20. Meza *La conciencia . . . , op. cit.,* pp. 268ff. See also Eyzaguirre, *Idario . . . , op. cit.,* p. 125; Encina, *op. cit.,* Vol. VI, p. 18; and John F. Bannon and Peter M. Dunne, *Latin America: an Historical Survey* (Milwaukee: The Bruce Publishing Co., 1947), p. 328.

21. Enrique Santibáñez, *Historia de la América Latina* (New York: D. Appleton and Co., 1918), p. 142.

22. Eyzaguirre, *Idario . . . , op. cit.,* p. 125.

Chile that had been so closely interrelated with the success of institutional authoritism started to disappear.[23]

The four traditional colonial centers of power—the governor, the *audiencia,* the *cabildo,* and the Church—were almost immediately reduced to two. A polarization of forces took place around the creole and peninsular groups and the different solutions that they proposed for dealing with the the new situation.[24] The *audiencia* and the Church saw their political influence reduced.[25] Representing respectively the two most important antagonistic elements, the creole aristocracy and the Spanish merchants and bureaucrats,[26] the *cabildo* of Santiago and the governor became the two centers of power.

In the struggle between these two for control of the country, the governor was definitely the weaker con-

23. It is interesting to observe that the same process of political disintegration was taking place in Spain. It is also significant that the development of Spain thereafter has not differed in any considerable degree from what could be considered a "typical Latin American patern." On the similarities of the political development of Spain and Hispanic America during the nineteenth century see Rafael Altamira y Crevea, "La historia de las instituciones políticas y civiles de América en la Universidad de Madrid," in *La Reforma Social,* Vol. III, No. I (Diciembre, 1914), pp. 5ff.

24. Some writers have argued that the political power of the *audiencia* and the Church actually began to diminish as a result of the Bourbon policies and governmental philosophy. For an exposition of this interpretation see Luis Sánchez Agesta, *El pensamiento político del despotismo ilustrado* (Madrid: Instituto de Estudios Políticos, 1953).

25. The *audiencia* was dismissed April, 1811. On the diminishing powers of the Church see Encina, *op. cit.,* Vol. VI, pp. 247f.

26. Meza, *La actividad . . . op. cit.,* p. 127. These two antagonistic groups are sometimes identified according to their different theoretical interpretations of the political situation. See Eyzaguirre, *Ideario . . . , op. cit.,* Vol. V, section 2. M.L. Amunátegui, *op. cit.,* pp. 172f., classifies them as responding to the Buenos Aires and the Lima influence.

tender, in part because of the personality of Francisco Antonio García Carrasco, who held office at that time. The way in which he had been appointed as well as his questionable political ability and moral integrity became added handicaps to his attempts to rally forces to his support. Governor García Carrasco was not a royal appointee. After the incumbent governor died in office, the military leaders of Concepción insisted that he be named successor and prevailed over the will of the *audiencia,* which had already designated someone else to fill the vacancy.[27] The new governor had been deeply involved in one of the most notorious scandals of colonial days, the Scorpion affair, and was believed to have taken an active part in the robbery of that ship's merchandise and the murder of its captain. These circumstances contributed, of course, to the low esteem in which he was held in the country.[28]

Independence

The deposition of the king altered the character of the governorship since the governor became the mere representative of new political institutions whose claims to power were questionable and whose physical integrity was challenged. Although he had the active cooperation of royal colonial officials and Spanish merchants, he could not subdue the militant antagonism of the creoles. Above all, the governor lacked a military force, the only instrument that could sustain him in power against the wishes

---

27. This military intervention in the political life of the colony could, perhaps, be used to support the theory that actual deterioration of the empire began with the Bourbon dynasty.
28. For an account of the governorship of García Carrasco and the Scorpion affair see Barros Arana, *op. cit.,* Vol. VIII, Chapters I and II.

of the *cabildo*.[29] It was not surprising, then, that the *cabildo* began to move steadily in the direction of total control without encountering any effective opposition.[30]

By 1810 a new power structure was evident as the creole aristocracy, which held most of the country's wealth and could muster the help of its workers, became the dominant force. The creoles demanded the resignation of Governor García Carrasco through the *cabildo*, and threatened to advance over the city if he refused. The members of the *cabildo*, in a show of strength, assembled approximately three thousand men around the capital.[31] These forces were overwhelmingly superior to the total of three hundred and ten men—two hundred infantrymen from Concepción, fifty dragoons of the Queen, and sixty artillerymen—commanded by the governor.

In the face of this ultimatum, the *audiencia* decided to ask for his resignation and to dismiss him if he refused. After consultation with the *oidores* and his municipal military chiefs, the governor accepted the recommendations of the *audiencia*.[32] Then the creoles maneuvered executive power into the hands of a junta. The continuation of the European conflict and the uncertainty concerning the future of Spain convinced them that this was the best solution.[33]

A junta was formed during the *cabildo abierto*[34] held

---

29. The army—as well as the Church—divided into two factions. For a description of how this division took place see Galdames, *A History* . . . , *op. cit.*, pp. 150f.
30. Meza, *La actividad* . . . , *op. cit.*, p. 127.
31. *Ibid.*, *pp.* 121f.
32. *Ibid.*, pp. 122f.
33. Villalobos, *op. cit.*, p. 225
34. The *cabildo abierto* has sometimes been referred to as a democratic institution, but at no point did it have such a character in the Spanish-American colonies. See Jerónimo Bécker, *La*

on September 18, 1810.[35] The composition of the junta resulted from an attempt to strike a balance between the different political forces of the moment.[36] The new government of the colony was formed with Mateo de Toro Zambrano as president of the junta, and José Antonio Martínez, the elected bishop of Santiago, vice-president; they supposedly stood for the traditional influence of the Crown and the Church respectively. Fernando Marquez de la Plata represented the peninsulars who were in favor of the junta. Juan Martínez de Rozas represented the creoles of Concepción, and José Ignacio de la Carrera those of Santiago. [37] Once in operation, the junta eliminated the *audiencia* from the political scene and reduced the power of the Church.

From its inception, the junta declared loyalty to Fernando II, but although its loyalty was probably sincere, the events taking place in Spain, as well as the internal situation of Chile, soon corroded the official links with the mother country.[38] Not until 1813 was there any definite talk about severing ties with Spain and actual independence was not proclaimed until February 2, 1818. These dates refer only to the public expression and legal formulation of the desire to form a new nation. In fact, independence began for Chile the very moment the Crown was removed. The colony became independent

_____

    política española en las Indias (Madrid: Imprenta de Jaime Retás Martín, 1920), p. 41; and Haring, *op. cit.,* p. 172.

35. For a detailed description of this historic meeting and the people who participated in it see Raúl Silva Castro, *Asistentes al Cabildo Abierto del 18 de septiembre de 1810* (Second Edition; Santiago: Academia de la Historia, 1960).

36. Villalobos, *op. cit.,* p. 235.

37. Castedo, *op. cit.,* Vol. I, p. 499.

38. Meza, *La actividad . . . ,* *op. cit.,* p. 82; and Barros Arana, *op. cit.,* Vol. VIII, p. 246.

de facto long before the *de jure* declaration and the inauguration of republican institutions.

The seizure of power by the *cabildo* degenerated into political chaos as a struggle developed among the creole forces. In the absence of any compromising tradition and upon the breakdown of the monarchical symbol of authority, the anarchical tendencies latent in the country soon found political expression.[39] The inability of the creoles in control of the junta to find a proper substitute for the role played by the Spanish Crown made it impossible to preserve political stability. As has been so aptly stated: ". . . independence from the metropolis and internal disintegration were the same thing since both yielded to the same escape from the center of gravity."[40]

The creation of a governing junta that would require an internal balance of diverse forces for survival demanded that the Chileans accept attitudes and conceptions of political self-restraint and equilibrium alien to their political culture. Chilean political life had, historically, always been based upon submission to a single center of authority with the monopoly of legitimacy. The inhabitants of the country had for centuries responded to this authoritistic tradition. The failure of attempts to institute a government that markedly departed from familiar patterns was logical and understandable. The cultural orientations of the population precluded a positive response to any nonauthoritistic scheme of political organization. The integrative character of the human mind forbade a positive reaction to nonauthoritistic political formulas

---

39. For a description of some of the anarchical tendencies which afflicted the colonists see de Madariaga, "El auge . . .", *op. cit.*, Vol. I, pp. 1359ff.

40. Eyzaguirre, *Fisonomía . . . , op. cit.*, p. 93.

so long as the traditional orientation remained unchanged.[41]

Obviously the new country had to be built with the
same people who were there before independence, and
their political attitudes could not be changed by the
stroke of the pen or the desire of the intellect. Force could
coerce the Chileans into behaving in a certain manner,
but such a remedy was superficial and temporary. Political
violence could not erase psychological and cultural inclinations. A military leader could achieve control, but
he could not create authority. If he were a charismatic
leader he could command personal allegiance, but with
his passing no institutional basis would remain on which
to develop a stable government. The attempt to bring
about permanent stabilization of the country through
the use of force involved a gross underestimation of perhaps subtle, but ultimately vital, cultural and psychological factors.

A culture is here understood as the expression of
traditional characteristics present in a given community.[42]
Whether these characteristics are universal or local, in-
stinctual or environmental, would not change the fact
that their existence is the expression of operative forces,
and that unless changes, or symptoms of change, are detected in the operative mechanism of the community,
there would be no reason to expect alterations of the

41. Kardiner, *op. cit.,* p. 421. This author discusses the characteristics of social change and the integrative quality of the human
mind asserting that "human beings show little capacity to alter
adaptive modes once they are established."
42. For a highly perceptive discussion of culture as an analytical
concept see David Bidney, *Theoretical Anthropology* (New
York: Schocken Books, 1967), pp. 373ff. For a somewhat different approach to the study of culture see Marvin Harris,
The Nature of Cultural Things (New York: Random House,
1964).

prevailing patterns of behavior. However, this is not to say that cultural traditions create by themselves inexorable patterns of behavior from which deviations are not possible.

Civil War

The groups that favored a retention of the political links with Spain did not give up after the governor was forced to resign and the creole-controlled junta was formed. They gained the active support of the vice-royalty of Peru, which had remained loyal to the Spanish government, and began to battle openly those who wanted the junta. Plagued by internal disputes and lack of discipline, the creoles succumbed to the troops dispatched by the viceroy. From October 1814 to January 1817 the country was back in Spanish hands.[43] Not until San Martín's famous incursion did the creoles regain control of Chile.

Usual reference to this armed conflict as a "war of independence" with definite creole and peninsular interests blurs comprehension of the actual nature of the war. It is necessary to bear in mind that the forces engaged in the fight where by no means homogeneous. There were many peninsulars who fought in support of the creole-dominated junta and a large number of Chileans who fought on the opposite side.[44] The creole aristocracy, traditionally represented in the cabildo and as having control of the first junta, did not encompass all the Chilean-born; the interests of the native upper class were not

43. This short period of Spanish domination is known as the "Reconquest." For a detailed account see Miguel Luis Amunátegui and Gregorio Victor Amunátegui, La reconquista española (Santiago: Imprenta Litografía i Encuadernación "Barcelona," 1912).

44. Alemparte, op. cit., p. 14.

shared by all creoles. Nor did the Spanish officials and merchants who strongly supported the governor's position and thus objected to the creation of the junta, represent all the peninsular inhabitants of the colony. Armed strife was not a clear-cut case of Spaniards against Chileans, foreigners versus natives. This interpretation has resulted from the erroneous conception that the independence of the country—and of the rest of Latin America—sprang from a great revolution. Much to the contrary, what did develop was essentially a non-revolutionary civil war. Enrique D. Bandía has explained the true character of the colonial wars:

> . . . there was no revolution against Spain, but rather, civil war among those who claimed a greater and better right to govern in the name of Fernando VII. This civil war . . . was not related to the revolts and popular movements which had taken place in Spain and America in preceding centuries, and which were directed toward changing abusive customs, policies, excessive taxes, or the unwelcome orders of hated officials.[45]

The breakdown of the authoritistic political system accomplished the removal of the procedural devices for solving conflicts and incited the different parts of the colonial political apparatus to struggle for total power.

---

45. *Napoleón y la independencia de América* (Buenos Aires: Ediciones Antonio Zamora, 1955), p. 260. The theory that the Hispanic American wars of independence were actually civil conflicts is accepted in relation to Chile by Encina, Eyzaguirre, Alemparte, M.L. Amunátegui, and Castedo among others. Castedo emphasizes the proper understanding of this fact when he explains that "fundamental historical phenomenon at the beginning of our independence is the character of civil war which it acquired immediately after the fight began."

Independence was simply the consequence of the situation created by the dissolution of effective Spanish rule.

It can be safely assumed that the armed conflict in Chile after 1810 did not originate in any desire to "liberate" the country from Spanish rule. Such an appraisal of the causes of this disturbance emerged after independence. Then, in search for symbols that would assert national pride and promote cohesion, the myth of the "revolutionary" war was integrated into the political folklore of the country.[46]

Caudillismo

Beginning with the establishment of the first governing junta, Chile experienced political anarchy and instability.[47] Under these circumstances, which supplied vast opportunities for the exercise of strong leadership, the powerful characters of Juan Martínez de Rozas and José Miguel Carrera made themselves felt. They were, in their country, the first manifestations of the caudillistic phenomenon. Among peoples long accustomed to respond to authoritistic symbols, a strong personality could elicit a high degree of acceptance and loyalty.

Within the Spanish political tradition, *caudillismo* was an effort to fill the vacuum left by the removal of the symbol of institutional authoritism. *Caudillismo* was an attempt, based upon charisma, to keep political forces under control by promoting allegiance to the person of the leader.

---

46. The character of the colonial fight is better understood when it is realized that events occuring in Spain at the same time were also produced by the collapse of the authoritistic system.
47. For a description of the first insurrection, known as the "Motín de Figueroa," which took place under the new system see Diego Barros Arana, *Historia general de la independencia de Chile* (Santiago: Imprenta Chilena, 1854), pp. 138ff.

Caudillismo, thus, is not to be confused with military control. The former can create legitimacy; the latter cannot. Allegiance would render the use of violence unnecessary. The employment of force is indicative of the failure to secure allegiance.[48] *Caudillismo* is a noninstitutional way of satisfying the authoritistic orientation latent in a country's political culture. Due to its reliance on individual leadership, the caudillistic solution tends to be temporary. The *caudillo* can be challenged by another charismatic leader, or be deposed by a militant minority free of his spell. And even if he were successful in retaining control, his existence is limited. Once he is dead, the legitimacy built upon allegiance to his person would tend to disappear. But despite its temporary nature, *caudillismo* is more conducive to stability than dictatorial (illegitimate) rule. The caudillistic solution is basically legitimate and thus acceptable whereas dictatorial rule rests upon coercion and its reliance on force is indicative of inability to attain allegiance. Although itself unstable, caudillistic leadership may, under propitious circumstances, contribute to the development of institutional authoritism.

The chaos-dictatorship chain reaction that followed independence was a logical outcome of the inability of the Chileans to replace properly the functions once performed by the Spanish monarch by developing institutional authoritism. Anarchy thus reigned until someone gained military control of the situation. But this control was usually shaky, and the example of a barracks revolt, especially if successful, would encourage similar actions by subordinates. In the initial years of its independent life, emanci-

48. See the distinction made between authority and power by Lasswell and Kaplan, *op. cit.,* p. 133.

pation meant for Chile a deadly cycle of political anarchy
and dictatorship.

Republican Anarchy

After San Martín's refusal to assume the government
of Chile, Bernardo O'Higgins, a native general and the
protégé of the Argentine hero, became the ruler of the
country, under the title of Supreme Director. Peace and
order did not accompany the victory over the enemy;
the struggle for power merely took a new form. The rule
of O'Higgins did not bring stability to the country because he did not offer the kind of leadership that, in the
absence of a pluralistic conception of government, could
evoke widespread acceptance and loyalty. Lacking charismatic qualities and incapable of exercising effective military control, he could not save his country from the
political chaos in which it was immersed. The honest
and courageous O'Higgins failed to provide Chile with
the authoritistic rule the country's cultural and political
traditions had established as prerequisites for a stable
regime. He did not realize the country's need for "an
active, energetic and demanding power."[49]

Self-rule did not mean order. The southern regions
were infected with bands of robbers who claimed to be
fighting for idealistic causes. Murder, rape, assault, and
every type of depravity ran rampant in many sections of
Chile.[50] In January, 1823 General O'Higgins was forced
out of power by a revolt led by General Freire who, after
boasting publicly that under no circumstances would he

---

49. Castedo, *op. cit.,* Vol. II, p. 749.
50. For an account of this situation see Benjamin Vicuña Mackenna, *La guerra a muerte: memorias sobre las últimas cam-
pañas de la independencia de Chile* (Santiago: Imprenta
Nacional, 1868).

become chief of state, promptly accepted the office.[51] The followers of O'Higgins, now in the opposition, turned conspirators. In 1824 the title of Supreme Director was replaced by that of President of the Republic, but this nominal change brought no effective result. Conspiracies, revolutions, and insurrections took their normal course. Presidents, congresses, and ministers came and went with astonishing facility.

Constitutions followed the same order of things. The first constitutional attempt was made in 1811 and subsequent charters were enacted in 1812, 1814, 1822, 1823, and 1828.[52] The problems of the country did not respond, however, to the constitutional treatment. Reality stubbornly refused to submit to laws. The beautifully written phrases about order, freedom, peace, and submission to government had no significant impact on the political behavior of the Chileans.[53]

Legislation and constitutional devices were used as quasi-magical formulas, which enactment, it was hoped, would end specific evils. In order to cure the political ills of Chile, it was thought sufficient to find the proper

---

51. In his manifesto to the country of December 12, 1822, General Freire said: "I assure you that I will never put the arms down until all Chileans are convinced that I am the greatest lover of their liberty. . . . I declare solemnly, in front of the people, that I will never occupy the chair of president. Neither are my forces sufficient for such a burden nor do I desire it. This declaration shall be the guarantee of my intentions." For the full text see Castedo, *op. cit.*, Vol. II, p. 756.

52. The full texts of these documents are reproduced in Ramón Briseño, *Memoria histórico-crítica del derecho público chileno* (Santiago: Imprenta de Julio Belín y Cía., 1949), pp. 266ff.

53. Alberto Edwards Vives, *La fronda aristocrática* (Fifth Edition, Santiago: Editorial del Pacífico, S.A., 1959), p. 42; and Ramón Sotomayor Valdés, *Historia de Chile bajo el gobierno del General D. Joaquín Prieto* (Santiago: Imprenta "Esmeralda," 1900), Vol. I, p. 23.

legal ingredients, to mix them in the right proportion, and to apply them swiftly.[54]

In line with this interpretation, repeated efforts were made to adopt ideas and institutions alien to the traditions and practices of the country. American and British institutions, as well as French ideas, were imitated in the hope they would produce in Chile the results they had elicited in their countries of origin.[55] An example of an attempt to mold behavior through the enactment of legal provisions was Article 249 of the constitution of 1823.

> Included in the legislation of the state will be the moral code that will detail the duties of the citizen at all ages and in all states of his social life, thus forming in him habits, exercises, duties, rituals, and pleasures that would *transform the law into customs* and the customs into civic and moral virtues.[56]

---

54. It is necessary, if we are to understand Chilean, and Latin American, political development, to notice the magic quality of law in the area. It has traditionally been looked upon not as a reflection of any preceeding reality, but as a way of quickly implementing idealistic conceptions. Void of pragmatic outlook and empirical traditions, Latin Americans have found easy escape from their political troubles in the enactment of legal instruments which, they hoped, would eventually transform reality. The psychological implications of this phenomenon have never been, to my knowledge, systematically investigated.

55. The tendency to copy foreign legal and political formulas and the attempt to mold the life of the nation according to them, is not peculiar to Chile but is characteristic of Spain and the Spanish American world in general. This phenomenon, that could be described as *lack of political originality,* is closely related to the most basic patterns of Latin American political behavior. Mario García Kohly, *El problema constitucional en las democracias modernas* (Madrid: Renascimiento, 1931), pp. 62f., sees it as the cause of many Latin American political problems.

56. Italics mine.

The belief that behavior could be transformed by law gained ground during the years of political anarchy. Constitutional sorcery, however, failed to lead the country out of its desperate situation and Chile was propelled along the same disorderly path the rest of the newly emancipated Spanish colonies had followed.[57] The situation led Juan Egaña, one of the most prominent intellectual figures of early republican life, to ask for the creation of institutions more in tune with the past of the nation. In his essay about the best system of government, he described the kind of executive required:

> The executive power should exercise absolute control over the administration, without the legislative bodies doing anything but providing a few permanent laws, and meeting shortly, and with long recess periods in between those meetings. This is necessary in order to give vitality and respect to the executive.[58]

The above judgement would seem justified by the success that presidential authoritism achieved in Chile after 1830 when legitimate executive predominance and political stability travelled together for a few decades. Such a development in nineteenth-century Chile would tend to lend validity to the assumption that a certain relationship must exist between stable political institutions and the psychological and cultural reality of a given community.

---

57. See the comments of Casimiro Albano as quoted in Galdames, *La Historia* . . . , *op. cit.*, Vol. I, pp. 768f.
58. *Ocios filosóficos y poéticos en la Quinta de las Delicias* (Londres: Impreso por D. Manuel Calero, 1829), p. 69. See also Camilo Henríquez, *Ensayo acerca de las causas de los sucesos desastrosos de Chile* as quoted in M.L. Amunátegui, *La alborada política de Chile después del 18 de septiembre de 1810* (Santiago, n.d.), p. 49; and Villalobos, *op. cit.*, p. 238.

IV.

The Restoration of Legitimate Rule

Enclosed in a narrow strip of land lying between the Andean mountains and the Pacific Ocean, Chile was, at the beginning of the nineteenth century, a small and thinly populated country. The Chileans inhabited a reduced space, singularly homogenous in population, climate, and economic production. The country was geographically isolated, economically uniform, and, in general, well articulated.[1] Even the failure to conquer the Araucanian Indians proved to be a unifying factor since it obviated the problem of assimilating a large, different ethnic group into national life. The great majority of the population lived in or near the central valley that goes from Coquimbo to the Bío-Bío river. Santiago and, to a lesser extent, Concepción were the two centers of social and political activities. Although a certain degree of regional feeling had prevailed in the southern city since colonial days, regionalism was to play only a minor part in Chilean politics.

---

1. Edwards, *La organización* . . . , *op. cit.*, pp. 34f.; Castedo, *op. cit.*, Vol. I, p. 77; and Frías, *op. cit.*, Vol. I, p. 148.

Economically, the country depended upon agricultural production, thus the land-owning class of the central valley controlled the economy. After independence their hold was almost total. No energetic mercantile or enterpreneur group in a position to challenge the economic predominance of the landed gentry existed in Chile.[2] The traditional favorable connotation that ownership of land brought with it added strength to the position of the landed aristocracy. Economic and geographic conditions also helped to establish and preserve aristocratic control. Upon dissolution of the old system, the Chilean wealthy class became a foremost political force.[3] The long series of fights and conflicts that plagued the independent life of the country from its inception took place largely among the members of the dominant class: ". . . they were sectors of the same class fighting each other."[4]

Economic uniformity, geographic homogeneity and isolation, and the obvious preponderance of one social class, all favored internal unity. These factors could not by themselves, however, bring internal stability to the nation. They could, under proper circumstances, facilitate control but they could not automatically produce stable government. Imposed order could expedite the establishment of a stable regime, but it could not create it. The relatively high degree of internal unity and uniformity that Chile possessed were thus only potential tools for the reestablishment of a stable system of government.

Awareness of the necessity to fill the vacuum left by the removal of Spanish authoritism increased in Chile

---

2. Julio Heise, *150 años de evolución institucional* (Santiago: Editorial Andrés Bello, 1960), p. 20.
3. Eyzaguirre, *Fisonomía . . . , op. cit.,* pp. 100f.
4. Heise, *op cit.,* p. 20.

under the pressure of the chaos and instability that succeeded independence. The failure of the nation to respond adequately to the non-authoritistic principles and institutions that had been borrowed from countries with different political traditions and customs testified to the deep Chilean commitment to authoritistic patterns.

The constitutions of 1812, 1814, 1818, and 1822 recognized the need for a strong and highly centralized executive,[5] but essentially the powers ascribed to it were designated within a pluralistic structure of political authority. This attempt to depart from the traditional authoritistic conception proved, in practice, incapable of ending the disorganization and political anarchy then prevalent in the country. The attainment of independence had not in any meaningful way changed the basic characteristics and orientations of the inhabitants of Chile. Constitutional changes could not alter the reality of the country's ways, traditions, and inclinations.[6]

The early dictatorial attempts of Martínez de Rozas, Carrera, O'Higgins, and Freire proved unable to replace the departed Crown in its ancient role of absolute theoretical ruler. A regime of force could subdue the country for a certain period of time, but it could not by itself elicit acceptance from the nation. Violence does not produce allegiance. The order it produces tends to be precarious. The distinction between power based upon coercion and power based upon authority was easily observable in the new country's early life. Thus, the first Chilean governments were unable to bring about stable rule. Dictatorship—that is, illegitimate rule based on coercion—tends, by definition, to be unstable.

5. *Ibid.*, p. 28.
6. Alberto Edwards Vives, *La organización política de Chile, 1810-1833* (Santiago: Editorial del Pacífico, S.A., 1955), p. 115. See also Heise, *op. cit.*, p. 13; and Briseño, *op. cit.*, p. 41.

The Civil War of 1829–1830

The civil conflict in which Chile was immersed during the years 1829 and 1830 started as just one more episode in the long series of anarchical events that had become the plight of the nation after secession from Spain. When General Freire resigned in 1827, General Francisco Antonio Pinto became acting president of Chile. He was a member of the liberal[7] group that desired to transform Chile into a democratic republic. The ill-fated federalist experiment of 1826 prompted the new president to convene a constitutional assembly that would draw once again a fundamental charter. The liberal-dominated assembly produced a document in which the only concession to the conservatives was the retention of Catholicism as the official religion. In general, the new constitution emerged as a blend of liberal and federalist ideas, possibly motivated by high ideals, but once more hopelessly out of tune with the reality of the country. The gravest fault of the new constitutional document was that "it trusted in the fallacy that laws can mold people."[8]

Under the new charter, elections for congress and the presidency were called for 1829. The selection of congressmen took place at the beginning of the year without any major incident. The liberals' won a handsome victory, and the presidential election was scheduled later in the year. General Pinto was the candidate of the group in power, but when it became common knowledge

---

7. The liberals were referred to by their opponents as *pipiolos,* or novices, because of the scant social prestige of the members of this group. In turn, the conservatives were branded as *pelucones* or "bigwigs," calling to mind the powdered wigs worn by colonial aristocrats on official occasions.

8. Galdames, *A History . . . , op. cit.,* p. 234. See also Ricardo Donoso, *Las ideas políticas en Chile* (México City: Fondo de Cultura Económica, 1946), pp. 98f.; and Heise, *op. cit.,* p. 29.

that he did not intend to assume office if elected, the vice-presidential election acquired great importance. The candidate of the government was Francisco Ruíz Tagle, a member of the party in power and Minister of Finances of the government, who became increasingly identified with the opposition group. The liberals did not fully recognize the peril until the election for presidential electors had been held. The government immediately sent orders to the electors it controlled to vote for Joaquín Vicuña instead of for Ruíz Tagle. The action came too late. The opposition had taken full advantage of the situation and had instructed its electors to vote for Ruíz Tagle.[9]

The 1828 constitution provided that from among those who had obtained votes for president, a president and a vice-president would be elected. Every presidential elector was alloted two votes. Thus, the vice-presidency would go to the candidate with the second largest amount of votes provided they constituted a majority of the total number of electors. In the event that no one but the successful presidential candidate should receive an absolute majority, the constitution provided for the election of the vice-president by congress from among those having an "immediate majority."[10] In the presidential election of 1829, with 201 presidential electors casting their votes, the results were as follows: General Pinto, 122 votes; Ruíz Tagle, 100 votes; General Joaquín Prieto, 61 votes; and Vicuña, 48 votes.[11]

---

9. Castedo, *op cit.,* Vol. II, Chapter XXIV.
10. For the provisions governing these elections see *Constitución política de la República de Chile promulgada el 8 de agosto de 1828,* Título VII, Artículos 71-74.
11. There were five other candidates who also obtained votes: Argomedo, 33; Rivera, 11; Infante, 8; Benavente, 7; and Solar, 6. For a description of this election see Castedo, *op cit.,* Vol. II, p. 815.

Since only the president elect, Pinto, received a majority of votes, the selection of the vice-president was referred to congress. Dominated by the liberals, congress declared Joaquín Vicuña vice-president and, as a result, the opposition immediately claimed that by passing over the candidates with the two largest pluralities, Ruíz Tagle and Prieto, congress had violated the constitution. The legislative organ maintained it was acting within its constitutional prerogative. In the name of legality and constitutionality, General Prieto took to arms in Concepción and, also in the name of legality and constitutionality, the government undertook military preparations against him. The fighting was on again. The constitution of 1828 and all the ideals and hopes in which it had originated gave way to cruel reality. The southern army advanced toward the capital without encountering much resistance. In Ochagavía, not far from Santiago, a battle took place between the army of Prieto and the forces loyal to the government. With the military outcome still undecided, a pact was signed by the contending factions that gave provisional control of the government and the military to ex-dictator Freire.[12] After an initial acceptance of this arrangement, which virtually did away with the liberal government, the conservatives decided that they could do without Freire. They had distrusted his past association with the liberals and also feared his political ambitions. Freire did not take his dismissal easily. He quickly embarked for Coquimbo where, in the name of legality and constitutionality, he soon organized an army to combat the conservative forces now in control of the government in Santiago. On April 17, 1830 Freire and his opponents came face to face near a small river named Lircay. Freire

---

12. A governing junta was formed composed of General Freire, Ruíz Tagle and Juan Agustín Alcalde.

was defeated and the conservatives became firmly entrenched in power.[13]

The Reestablishment of Law and Order

The civil war that ended in the battle of Lircay marked a turning point in the history of Chile. The transformation occurring in the political life of the nation was of such magnitude that it has been said, "after 1830 one is reading the history of a different country."[14]

What happened in Chile after 1830 that could justify such a comment? A reaction against the multiple attempts to organize the country according to ideas and institutions that were alien to the nation's history and cultural tradition gained momentum. For the first time since the Spanish rule collapsed, the need to create a strong center of political authority that could effectively be adjusted to the authoritistic orientation of the country was officially recognized.

> The idea that had been gaining force since the battle of Lircay was that the Constitution should be reformed and that absolutely no attention should be paid to theoretical principles; instead attention should be paid to cultural and economic factors, and to social needs.[15]

If the country were to be stabilized and order restored, the political institutions would have to be in accordance with the nature of the society. The customs and traditions of the colonial past offered the basis for the solution of the political crisis that the country had

---

13. Galdames, *A History* . . . , *op. cit.*, pp. 234ff.; and Castedo, *op. cit.*, Vol. II, Chapter XXIV.
14. Edwards, *La fronda* . . . , *op. cit.*, p. 45.
15. Donoso, *op. cit.*, p. 104.

endured for twenty years. The road to peace and order was an authoritistic one. The alternative was chaos. The victors of Lircay were probably intellectually unaware of specific authoritistic principles of political organization, but they realized that if they were to reinstate legitimate civilian control of the government on firm grounds, their republican present had to be an extension of the colonial past so abruptly interrupted.[16]

The victory of the conservative troops brought a high degree of identification among the members of the aristocracy. The Chilean patricians, many of whom were theoretically in sympathy with liberal ideas, recognized the ill effects that had resulted from the attempts at political pluralization. They had to accept the fact that such efforts had been fruitless. Circumstances and self-interest, if nothing else, forced them to adopt a more practical attitude and to reduce their concern for theoretical forms.

The ability of the Chilean aristocracy to close ranks politically was, of course, in part due to the physical and economic characteristics of the country. The tight familial and social ties that linked the country's wealthy class with the army, clergy, and bureaucracy made coming to terms possible.[17]

Diego Portales

In the turmoil of the 1829–1830 civil war, a figure destined to cast a long shadow over the political development of his people emerged. Diego Portales was born in

---

16. Antonio Iñiguez Vicuña, *Historia del período revolucionario en Chile, 1848-1851* (Santiago: Imprenta del Comercio, 1906), p. 60.; Alberto Edwards Vives, *Bosquejo histórico de los partidos políticos chilenos* (Santiago: Ediciones Ercilla, 1936), pp. 22ff.; and Donoso, *op. cit.,* p. 107.
17. Galdames, *Historia . . . , op. cit.,* pp. 830f.

Santiago in 1793 of a distinguished creole family. He did not participate in the independence movement or become involved in the early republican struggle, but, instead, began his career as a businessman. The commercial firm of Portales, Cea and Company received from General Freire a monopoly on tobacco, liquors, and tea, but after two years the contract with the government was annulled. The liquidation of the operation was slow and complicated and it soon acquired political overtones. As a result, Portales found himself highly involved in partisan politics and soon became the leader of a highly articulate political faction. Through the publication of a newspaper, *El Hambriento,* in 1827, Portales gained considerable popularity for his attacks on the "pipiolo" government. When José Tomás Ovalle came into power during the conservative revolt of 1829, Portales was made a member of his cabinet. He simultaneously assumed the portfolios of interior and foreign relations as well as war and navy. As soon as he stepped into government, his energetic character and leadership qualities made him the real ruler of the country.[18]

Diego Portales had a precise idea of what principles of government he favored for Chile. He clearly saw the necessity for political order within a republican framework as the foundation upon which the political stability of the nation would have to be erected.[19] His belief in a highly centralized center of authority and power was so great, that he dismissed as useless any kind of legal device that would interfere with the implementation of this concept of government. There was no doubt in his mind

18. Galdames, *A History* . . . , *op. cit.,* pp. 236ff.
19. See his letter to J.M. Cea dated March 10, 1822 as quoted in Raúl Silva Castro, *Ideas y confesiones de Portales* (Santiago: Editorial del Pacífico, S.A., 1954), p. 15.

that if law came into conflict with effective governmental action, the latter should prevail.

> With the men of law it is very difficult to get along; under such circumstances, what the hell is the use of constitutions and papers if they are unable to remedy an evil everyone knows exists, or that is going to take place but that cannot be prevented by taking the necessary measures because one must wait until the crime had been committed? In Chile the law has no use other than to produce anarchy, absence of sanction, corruption, eternal fighting, nepotism. . . .[20]

It is necessary, though, in order to place Portales' ideas within proper perspective, to realize that his understanding of the law was a Spanish-Chilean one. He was attacking, above everything else, the idealistic, moralistic, and unreal laws and regulations that during the republican years had failed to contribute in any meaningful way to the improvement of the nation. Perhaps Portales' lack of intellectual sophistication rendered his judgement both crude and realistic.

As the all-powerful minister of Ovalle's government, Diego Portales did not waste any time putting his ideas into action. The military leaders were the first to feel his iron grip. Departing from what already constituted the republican custom of leniency toward revolutionary officers and mutinous leaders, Portales was bold and harsh in his treatment of anyone whose loyalty to the government was questionable. As a check on the army, a civic and national guard was established. The defeated liberals, together with all those who were not active supporters of the government, were denied admission to political offices. As soon as plots against the government were dis-

---

20. Letter of Diego Portales to A. Garfas dated December 6, 1834.

covered, Portales suppressed them implacably. Family
links and social position did not reduce the severity of the
punishment. The impunity granted to leaders of the
military and political revolts which had been based on
familial and social connections and permissiveness of the
official authorities—probably in the hope that equal treatment would be extended to them should their political
fortunes change—was ended after 1830. The minister
sought to transform the government into an effective and
respected institution. Revolts were not to be tolerated
regardless of whom the rebels were. Opposition writers
were quickly exiled and the whole country was rapidly
made conscious of the strong power exercised from Santiago. Although not the legal head of the government,
Portales became the undisputed ruler of the country and
decisively applied himself to the task of establishing a
powerful and well disciplined government.[21] In order to
achieve his purpose, he counted on the traditional forces
that had shaped the Chilean political scene for hundreds
of years.[22] In direct reference to this tradition, he coined

21. Agustin Edwards, *El alba: 1818–1841* (Valparaíso: Sociedad,
Imprenta y Litografía Universo, 1931), p. 244; and Donoso,
op. cit., p. 102.
22. Galdames, *A History . . . , op. cit.,* p. 239, explains the success
of Portales as follows:
It seems incredible that one man alone should have been
able to acquire such insuperable power in so short a time.
But when one recalls that colonial society had been accustomed to receiving orders from abroad and without discussion;
and bears in mind that no one had revealed more character
than he, nor more activity, nor more disinterestedness in
the exercise of his ministry; and when it is known that a long
period of anarchy had already made itself insupportable and
had even led some to despair of the fate of the republic, one
should not express surprise at the preference for a master who
could mold the government system with a steel-like energy,

his famous phrase: "In Chile, the social order has to be preserved by the weight of the night."[23]

Under the leadership of Portales, the landed gentry began to actively cooperate in the creation of a regime that could bring peace and order to their battered land. Irrespective of their own personal feelings toward the minister-dictator, the aristocratic forces soon perceived the basic character of his policies and rapidly understood how much they stood to gain from them.

The rule of Portales introduced some very important changes into the political organization of the country. For the first time since colonial days, Chile had an effective government.[24] The political ability and personal determination of the minister were greatly responsible for these developments, but they were not the only factors. Portales' attempt to bring about tight governmental control of the country could not have succeeded so swiftly had it not been for the geographic and sociological characteristics of Chile in those days. A small territory, easy communications, social homogeneity, and the absolute economic predominance of the landed elite facilitated the development of an effective, highly centralized and executive-controlled system of government.

On September 18, 1831, Joaquín Prieto was inaugurated president of Chile. Portales, although elected vice-president, had refused to accept his own election and resigned from the government a month before, claiming

rather for a multitude of men without sufficient will to cause another's to triumph.

It is interesting to note that this paragraph was omitted from the seventh edition of the Spanish original. See also Fernando Campos Harriet, *Historia constitucional de Chile* (Santiago: Editorial Jurídica de Chile, 1956), p. 208.

23. Letter to J. Tocornal dated July 16, 1832.
24. Edwards, *La organización . . . , op. cit.,* p. 105.

that he wanted to retire from politics. He moved to Valparaíso, but soon left and retired to an estate near the small town of Ligua. Although removed physically from the councils of government, Diego Portales remained a formidable political figure.[25] In the short period during which he had controlled the political destinies of the country, he had given Chile a dynamic and effective governmental apparatus. The new president could not afford to ignore the person responsible for the creation of the new order. President Prieto consulted Portales frequently and no important governmental action was taken without the knowledge, and approval, of the ex-minister and reluctant vice-president. In spite of his proclaimed desire to abandon public responsibilities, Diego Portales stayed very much in the center of political life, but not until 1835 did he again assume political office. As the presidential election drew near, some internal rivalries arose within the conservative group that threatened unity of the government. In September of 1835 Portales entered the cabinet, took up the two ministries he had held in 1830, and once again became the undisputed master of the country. The re-election of General Prieto had been assured.

The national crisis gave way to an international conflict that had been brewing since the day Bolivia and Peru became united in a confederation under dictator Santa Cruz. This international emergency made the presence of Portales in the government inevitable. Until his death on June 6, 1837, he maintained total control.

---

25. For a description of the political activities Portales undertook during these years see Ramón Sotomayor Valdés, *Historia de Chile durante los cuarenta años transcurridos desde 1831 hasta 1871* (Santiago: Imprenta de "La Estrella de Chile," 1875), Vol. I, pp. 369ff.

The Portalian Regime

The organizational work performed by Portales gave the government a greater degree of cohesiveness and efficiency than any prior republican regime had attained. By controlling the military and the country at large, he was able to supply the government with the proper tools to deal successfully with attempts to overthrow it. Some check could now be applied on the political forces that had run amok for twenty years. Portales accomplished this by strengthening the powers of the executive and by forcing the landed aristocracy to realize the advantages of the new state of affairs.

Revolts against the government did not cease to occur,[26] but now they stood less chance of success. The government was prepared to counter them and the personal risks involved in seditious activities rapidly increased. This new ability of the government to quell revolts effectively gave the nation a greater degree of internal order than it had known since independence. Portales himself was captured and murdered by some rebellious military officers, but they still failed in their attempt to overthrow the regime.[27] The principles upon which the Portalian structure had been laid were so well rooted in the Chilean mind that the death of its master builder did not destroy it.

The political regime that emerged in Chile after 1830 was characterized by the predominant role played by the executive. It was Portales' objective to increase both the actual power and the prestige of the president. As a caudillistic leader in effective command of the gov-

---

26. Galdames, *A History* . . . , *op. cit.,* p. 256.
27. A description of the revolt that caused Portales' death is given in Sotomayor, *Historia de Chile bajo* . . . , *op. cit.,* Vol. II, Chapters XXVIII to XXXII.

ernment, he tried to remodel the presidential office. He envisioned the presidency as a symbol of unity and the recipient of national allegiance and seems to have wanted to recreate, under republican garb, the basic forms of institutional authoritism.

As long as Diego Portales lived, however, his work toward the institutionalization of stable political authority could not be successfully concluded. His caudillistic personal qualities made him, not the president, the symbol of respect and recipient of allegiance. Under his rule, the legitimation of governmental control had been based not on traditional but charismatic grounds. It was only after his sudden murder that institutional authoritism returned to Chile. After Portales' death, the president became the only source of political authority and the final arbiter of disputes. The chief executive started at this point "to absorb everything and became the center of the nation's political life."[28]

Reality and Law: The Constitution of 1833

Diego Portales had not been the first to advocate a return to authoritistic principles as the solution for the political problems of his land. Many other Chileans had harbored similar ideas, and they found expression in some of the clauses of the many constitutions enacted since independence. But it was not until after 1830 that the reinstitutionalization of absolute executive supremacy, under republican forms, was possible. The mere constitutional recognition of the need for presidential supremacy did not have the power to produce such a development. Written regulations could not make a president powerful unless there were some real bases for the develop-

---

28. Donoso, *op. cit.*, p. 112.

ment and exercise of the legally ascribed powers. Portales helped to create presidential supremacy in reality by restructuring the governmental machinery. After this was accomplished, laws could be of use in organizing and rationalizing the executive's functions. Then constitutional devices could assist in directing allegiance toward the office rather than toward the person occupying it. Such depersonalization of authority would be conducive to stable government.

Soon after assuming power, the conservatives went to work on a new constitution that would provide for the legal dictatorship of the president. By doing so, they paved the way for the developments that took place after Portales' assassination when, for the first time in republican Chile, the constitutional structure closely resembled the reality of the country.

In 1831 a constituent congress was convened for the purpose of revising the 1828 constitution. What started as a revision ended up as the enactment of a completely new document in May 1833. Those in control of the government felt that the charter of 1828 had not provided the chief executive with the legal means necessary for exercising total power. They thought this a major defect in the document and resolutely began to remedy it.[29] Under the new constitution the president was granted undisputed legal supremacy over the other branches of government. So wide was the range of powers vested upon the chief executive that an early critic of the constitution described the ensuing situation as follows:

---

29. See the speech delivered by President Prieto on September 18, 1841 in Sotomayor, *Historia de Chile bajo . . . , op. cit.,* Vol. IV, pp. 250f. The executive powers of this constitution were defined in Title VII, Articles 60-83.

A single citizen administering the state, only one individual exercising the rule of the whole nation: this is, in brief, the role represented by the President of Chile, according to our Constitution. . . . Thus, the title dedicated to that official announces from its very first words the immense amount of power vested in him. . . . It is necessary to observe, of course, that the president is not only the chief of the Executive Power, he is not only the supreme administrator of the State, he is also the first authority of the nation, he is its *Supreme Chief*. Thus, the Legislative Power . . . is well below him; and the same is true of the Judicial Power and of the Municipal Power; all these other Powers that the Constitution recognizes, and that science classifies as such, become mere subordinates, dependencies, almost subjects, of that immense Executive Power.[30]

The principle of executive supremacy that Diego Portales was trying to introduce into the political life of the country was now sanctioned by the constitution. Law moved a step closer to reality.[31] But it was after 1837 that the document came to correspond more to the actual

30. Manuel Carrasco Albano, *Comentarios sobre la constitución política de Chile de 1833* (Valparaíso: Imprenta y Librería del Mercurio, 1858), p. 121.
31. The president of the country in an address to the constitutional convention on October 20, 1831 thought it convenient to mention the need to consider the actual characteristics of the country for which they were legislating. "Remember at every minute that you are legislating for Chile, and that the goal of the laws is the happiness of man, and of nations, and not the proclamation of principles." See Sotomayor, *Historia de Chile durante . . .* , *op. cit.*, Vol. I, p. 229. It is quite interesting to note that although the president in this speech was making a call for a more "pragmatic" constitution, he still remained basically loyal to the traditional idealistic Spanish conception of law.

political reality than any other prior republican constitution.

The new constitution made the president legally omnipotent. He was, in fact, placed in a position similar to that enjoyed by the monarch before independence. Under the new legal arrangement, this position has been explained in the following way:

> In front of this Supreme Chief of the Nation so formidably equipped, nothing could stand. In fact, and without having to violate the legal formulas, the presidents were almost absolute monarchs.[32]

The new constitution provided for at least two apparent institutional checks on the powers of the president —congress and the electoral system. The president had, however, ways of rendering the restraining mechanisms unworkable by exercising tight control over both congressmen and their election. He had been granted the right to suspend individual guarantees and to use extraordinary powers. Also he could declare, in accord with a council of state in no position to resist his will, any province or the entire country in a state of siege. The exercise of these powers was actually "equivalent to a temporary suppression of the constitution."[33] But the political supremacy of the president was not constitutional in origin. The constitution reflected, and helped to insure, the strength the executive had acquired since 1830, and especially after 1837.[34] A strong and prestigious presidency

32. Edwards, *La organización* . . . , *op. cit.,* p. 130; for a provocative discussion of the 1833 constitution see pp. 114ff. On the same subject see Heise, *op. cit.,* pp. 37f.; and Galdames, *A History* . . . , *op. cit.,* pp. 240ff.

33. *Ibid.,* p. 241. See also Edwards, *La organizacón* . . . , *op. cit.,* pp. 130f.

34. Julio Ycaza Tigerino, *Sociología de la política hispanoamericana.* (Madrid: Seminaric de Problemas Hispanoamericanos,

emerged now as the center of the country's political life. Under the system of government inherited from Portales, it was not difficult for those occupying the presidential chair to rule the country in an absolute fashion. They became the accepted symbols of authority and were able to determine freely both the selection of their successors and the members of congress.[35] Actually, the president was subject to no effective checks at all. The political allegiance that for centuries had been paid to the Spanish monarch found republican expression. The development and acceptance of presidential supremacy had paved the way for a republican form of institutional authoritism.

The necessary legal machinery for the rationalization of presidential authoritism was contained in the constitution of 1833. Without such juridical paraphernalia, the process of legitimizing the new system might have been much more difficult. The constitution gave formal expression to ultimate executive power and in doing so, it helped to enhance the prestige and the acceptance of that same power. Despite its contribution to the system, it must be kept in mind that the new constitution did not create it.

Legally oriented analysts would tend to trace the roots of the new political situation to the written document. Such explanations are fallacious and preclude a proper understanding of the Chilean political life by over-emphasizing the creative value of legal devices. In all probability, the constitutional document would have ac-

---

1950), p. 261, believes that Diego Portales was not very interested in the constitution and only saw it as a way of placating those who deemed necessary some kind of overall legal organization. This author asserts that Portales' only interest was to avoid a type of constitution that would handicap realistic political action.

35. Castedo, *op. cit.*, Vol. II, pp. 881f.

complished very little had it been promulgated under different circumstances. The reorganization of the country's real political life induced by Portales together with the social, economic, and geographic conditions of Chile at the time, made the success of the new arrangement possible.

The constitutional allotment of power alone would probably not have been enough to build a strong and stable presidency. The constitutional prerogatives would have had to be rendered operational by the presidential possession of the necessary political instruments. Presidential authoritism became possible because there had been a predisposition in the Chilean political psyche to accept absolute monistic control,[36] and because Portales had done the necessary groundwork to make the presidency the beneficiary of this tendency. The constitution made it viable by giving expression under republican forms to the same patterns of political behavior that had been so much evidenced under colonial rule.[37]

---

36. Galdames, *A History* . . . , *op. cit.*, p. 242, describes this inclination as "the ingrained habit of the people of that time of obeying sovereign authority."

37. Alberto Edwards, *Páginas históricas* (Santiago: Editorial Difusión Chilena, 1945,) p. 48, ascribes the success of the new constitution to its being in tune with the country's character and past. "Thus, the makers of the 1833 Constitution created a Supreme Chief of the nation modeled after the memories of the colonial structure. Nothing could be more in line with the idiosyncrasy of the country than those things that the country was used to." See also Sotomayor, *Historia de Chile durante* . . . , *op. cit.*, Vol. I, p. 270. Alberdi, *op, cit.*, p. 156, thought that the Chilean example should have been followed by the rest of the Latin American countries. "Time has shown that the Chilean solution is the only rational one for republics that have recently been monarchies. Chile has made everybody see that between the absolute lack of government and dictatorship there is a regular form of government; and this system is that of a constitutional president who could assume the

The 1833 document became a useful component of the political order and legal continuity that followed the government of Portales.[38] After the Portalian experiment was accomplished, the anarchy and confusion of the preceeding years seemed to fade away. After twenty years of chaos and disorganization, Chile found its way back to political stability via authoritism.

The New Authoritism

Colonial patterns of political behavior proved important to the republican reorganization of the country, but this was not the result of some inevitable and abstract process of cultural or historical determinism. The possibility that a marked alteration in colonial political ways might have occured in Chile after independence should not be totally excluded. But the acceptance of such a possibility as probable could only result from inability to understand the cause-effect mechanism of Chilean political behavior, rather than from any positive indication that different patterns of conduct would have been more successful.

Notwithstanding the difficulties inherent in the prognostication of changes in social behavior, and accepting the assumption that the future is not determined by the past in an abstract deterministic fashion, it still would have to be accepted that the Chilean colonial behavior suggested the existence of powerful authoritistic ten-

---

faculties of a king . . . . I would not hesitate in asserting that the future of the South American states would depend upon the constitution of the executive power."

38. "The constitutional organization of Chile was that of a monarchy ruled by a president, and this was what, for more than half a century, preserved peace and progress in the country." Pío Alvarado Jaramillo, *El régimen totalitario en América* (Guayaquil: Editora Noticia, S.A., 1940), p. 104.

dencies in that society. Since the basic psychological, sociological, and cultural aspects of the colonial period had remained apparently unchanged after separation from Spain, it would be unwarranted to assume that the environment or the people were ready for major political changes.

Although the system of presidential supremacy that flourished after Portales' death was very similar in many important respects to the institutional authoritism of the Spanish monarchy, there were substantial differences between them. The colonial arrangement was highly conducive to the idealization of the royal functions. The personal qualities and characteristics of the monarch were obscured by the glitter and prestige of the office he occupied. Royal inaccessibility also contributed to the depersonalization of the monarchy and its functions. This situation was compounded by the fact that strict laws of succession minimized the possibility of competition for the office.

Under these circumstances, allegiance to the Spanish king during the colonial period meant, in fact, loyalty to the office and not to the person exercising it. This distinction was not, of course, an absolute one. A strong monarch could add to the prestige and influence of the Crown, and a weak one could procure some devotion to his person by the mere fact that he was sitting on the throne. Notwithstanding the political complexity of the interaction between the office and the person holding it, loyalty was primarily rendered to the institution in the Spanish authoritistic equation.

A system of presidential authoritism would by necessity lack some of the ingredients present in the Spanish system. A republican presidency was not as likely to be the subject of as much idealization as the colonial monarchy. The republican executive would be raised to his position by people who might be reluctant to consider him superior to them, and who would not, therefore, hesitate to challenge his rule under certain circumstances. A republican president would usually be denied the same degree of aloofness and detachment in which a royal prince could indulge. If anything, the president-to-be would be forced to engage in some sort of political competition before attaining the high office. Such competition, and the fact that he would seldom be the only one aspiring to the office, made his political position more vulnerable than that secured through the Spanish monarchical formula.

Allegiance to the president, although basically institutionalized after 1837, tended to retain a high degree of concern with the person of the ruler. Presidential authoritism developed as a blend of personal and institutional elements of loyalty. This state of affairs, this incomplete institutionalization of authoritism, demanded that the chief executive contribute a certain charismatic factor to the regime's stability. It is doubtful that under any circumstances a perfect institutionalization of authoritism is possible. Nevertheless, there are polarizing tendencies that make the system more or less caudillistic or institutional. Presidential authoritism began in Chile with a much higher degree of charisma, or caudillistic tendencies, than had been the case in Spanish colonial authoritism. This is quite important to keep in mind because the caudillistic-institutional ratio may affect the system's chances for continuity.

The newly acquired system offered the country a rare republican commodity in the recently independent Hispanic nations—political stability. The internal anarchical forces that had broken loose after the separation from

Spain now bowed to presidential authority. It is important to remember, however, as has already been mentioned, that these anarchical elements were not eradicated but merely checked and the control restraining them was not as thorough as it had been in colonial days.

Whatever disorderly political tendencies Chile possessed were so well ingrained in its social fabric that they could not be magically eliminated by political or legal action. Chile achieved stability not through the removal of the psychological or cultural roots of political disorder, but by controlling them through legitimate presidential supremacy.[39] The choice the Chileans faced was not between monistic rule and pluralistic government but between authoritism and chaos. Basically the same alternative simultaneously confronted Spain and her ex-colonies.

From almost the very moment the conservatives came into power, it was evident that the anarchical forces had been simply brought under control and not eliminated by Portales and the system he helped create. No fewer than five attempts to overthrow the government took place between the end of the 1829–1830 civil war and Portales' death.The period of the war against the Bolivian-Peruvian confederation (1836–1839) also saw its share of conspiracies, revolutions, and *pronunciamientos*.[40] Attempts to depose the established rule continued to occur, but after 1830 the government was in possession of effective tools

---

39. It is not uncommon among Chilean historians and writers to ascribe the orderly development of the country under the Portalian regime to racial uniformity and climatic conditions. This interpretation fails, of course, to properly account for the chaotic years of 1810 to 1830 since no appreciable differences in racial composition or climatic conditions can be established for that period.

40. Eyzaguirre, *Fisonomia . . . , op. cit.,* pp. 140ff., analyzes some of the disruptive tendencies that continued to operate under the new regime.

for dealing with such rebellious incidents—first, the effectiveness of the ubiquitous minister, and afterwards, the prestige and power of the presidential office.

After twenty years of chaos and bloody strife Chile began to find its way into stable political life. The newly-attained stability rested mainly on the shoulders of a president who came to perform many of the functions played in the past by the Spanish monarch. The country had begun to develop a system of government that apparently was in accord with its cultural inclinations, psychological constitution, and past history. The principles and practices that departed from the country's politics with the breakdown of Spanish colonial rule were reestablished in republican garb. Or as a Chilean analyst put it, the Portalian effort culminated in "the restoration of the colonial forms under an apparently republican structure."[41]

---

41. Julio César Jobet, *Ensayo crítico del desarrollo económico-social de Chile* (Santiago: Editorial Universitaria, S.A., 1955), p. 34.

V.

Deterioration and Breakdown of Presidential Supremacy

The years between 1831 and 1891 are commonly referred to by Chilean historians and political analysts as the "Portalian era." The grouping of these years under the same label tends to convey an idea of unity and similarity, the use of the "Portalian" adjective implying a certain connotation of executive predominance and stability. Such a classification is to a certain degree arbitrary—as are most historical generalizations—and Chilean historians have tried to remedy this by acknowledging the existence of two distinct "epochs" within the "era." Two periods are distinguished which are respectively identified as "autocratic" and "liberal."[1] Although not historically exact, this distinction should help to understand the political changes that took place in the country.

There are clear indications that after 1851 presidential authoritism began to falter in Chile. The increasing

---

1. Galdames, *A History . . .* , *op. cit.*, pp. 255 and 305, identifies the first period as the "Autocratic Republic" and the second as the "Liberal Republic."

117

use of violence and coercion on the part of the executive were indications of a weakening in the allegiance rendered to it. The deterioration of the system seems to have begun during the administration of President Manuel Montt.[2] At least, it was during his years in power, 1851 to 1861, that the first signs of malfunction appeared. Foreign pluralistic conceptions of government became popular among intellectuals; the united front presented by the economic elite started to break, and political parties[3] began to gain prominence.

The system of presidential authoritism that Portales established did not operate without difficulties. There were political forces that failed to conform to the new situation. To understand the deterioration and breakdown of presidential authoritism it would be necessary to analyze the character of the struggle that ensued and prod the nature of the conflicting elements. Then it would be possible to see how a political system that had profound psychological and cultural foundations was undermined and destroyed.

After the consolidation of presidential authority and power took place in 1837, Chilean political life acquired a strong element of stability. The support given to the

---

2. On the Montt administration see Alberto Edwards Vives, *El gobierno de Don Manuel Montt* (Santiago, 1936); Benjamín Vicuña Mackenna, *Historia de los diez años de la administración de Don Manuel Montt* (Santiago: Imprenta Chilena, 1862-1863); and Anon., *Cuadro histórico de la administración Montt escrito según sus propios documentos* (Valparaíso: Imprenta y Librería del Mercurio, 1861), p. 12.

3. Political parties existed in Chile previously, but they started to acquire a more dynamic character around 1849, and by 1861 had become familiar political instruments. For descriptions of the parties development see Alberto Edwards Vives, *Bosquejo . . . , op. cit.*; and René León Echaínz, *Evolución de los partidos políticos chilenos* (Santiago: Editorial Ercilla, 1939).

executive by the great majority of the politically influential groups and interests made presidential supremacy
overwhelming. There were, of course, for reasons that
have been touched upon in the preceeding chapter,
groups and individuals who took it upon themselves to
challenge the president.

From its very inception in Chile, presidential authoritism was unable to secure the wide and lasting obedience
given to the Spanish Crown. The ingredients for a high
degree of institutionalization were lacking. Whereas the
monarch had been primarily interested in over-all loyalty
and formal submission (hence, the *se acata pero no se
cumple* principle and the concomitant royal moderating
function), the president was much more directly concerned with the actual application of his orders. The king
could differentiate between disobedience and disloyalty,
but the president, as a rule, could not. The need for
direct presidential involvement was aggravated by the
increasing scope of governmental action and the extension of political activities to new layers of the population.

Notwithstanding these limitations, the Chilean presidency acquired widespread allegiance and wielded considerable, although not complete, authority and power.
The repeated failures of the regime's enemies bear witness
to the president's control over the country.

The administrations of Joaquín Prieto (1831–1841),
Manuel Bulnes (1841–1851), and Manuel Montt (1851–
1861) succeeded each other in perfect order, each president being elected for two consecutive five-year terms.
Although presidential authoritism began under Prieto,
during most of his time in office his authority and power
were second to Portales. Bulnes and Montt faced revolts
they were able to thwart. President Bulnes enjoyed a
tranquil and peaceful first term but encountered difficul-

ties during the second. In April 1851 there was an insurrectional attempt in the capital and in September uprisings took place in the towns of La Serena and Concepción. The later revolts were led by the defeated presidential candidate. President Montt, who was inaugurated while the 1851 insurrection was going on, was confronted with another armed rebellion in 1859.[4]

The process of laying the foundations for authoritistic rule had only started when the first of a long series of setbacks began. Symptomatic of this situation was Montt's inability to have his personal choice succeed him in office. The importance of this is demonstrated by the fact that the ability of the incumbent to choose his successor was both closely related to and symbolic of presidential supremacy.

Authoritistic rule was challenged primarily by ideas and concepts alien to Chilean cultural traditions and social-psychological characteristics. It should not be surprising that there were forces in the country and individuals able and willing to attempt a departure from traditional patterns of behavior. All cultures and societies probably have in their midst actual or potential advocates of ideas and concepts other than those in practice. Why and how the supporters of deviant modes gain ascendancy, and to what degree their ways are able to replace effectively the traditional ones is important to determine.

Lack of Originality

Out of the literary movement that took place in Chile around 1842, and under the heavy influence of

---

4. For a description of this revolutionary attempt see Pedro Pablo Figueroa, *Historia de la revolución constituyente, 1858-1859* (Santiago: Imprenta "Victoria" de H. Izquierdo y Cía., 1889).

French ideas,[5] an intellectual elite emerged. This new force was theoretically committed to pluralistic forms that would conflict with presidential authoritism. The desire to implement abstract pluralistic theories and principles of government started to gain support. As had been the case directly after independence, intellectual idealism became a militant political force.[6]

The desire of the intellectuals to identify themselves and their country with Europe and Western European ideas was not a phenomenon peculiar to Chile. The unwillingness of the intelligentsia to develop ideas and interpretations that would have responded to the reality of their nations is a characteristic present in all the Latin American countries.[7] This lack of originality that seems continuously to permeate the political—as well as the literary and artistic—life of the region is a most interesting and vexing problem.[8] Its causes are difficult to determine but its importance to the understanding of Chilean, and Latin American, political behavior is difficult to overestimate. It seems quite likely that the widespread imitation of European forms—the United States and the rest of the Western societies included—implies a tacit rejection of native patterns. The historical fact of small numbers of white colonists finding themselves in the midst of societies numerically controlled by Indians and Negroes might have created a psychological predisposition to

---

5. For a discussion of the French intellectual influence on Latin America see Ricardo Caillet-Bois, "La América española y la revolución francesa, in *Cursos y conferencias*, year IX, Vol. XVI, numbers 4 and 5 (July-August, 1940), pp. 164ff.
6. See Galdames, *A History* . . . , *op. cit.*, pp. 274ff.
7. Mexico after 1917 seems to be a partial exception to the rule.
8. I believe this tendency is present in a large number of other non-European societies. Its analysis should be challenging and rewarding and I hope to have the opportunity to deal with it at some length in the future.

imitate European, or white, patterns as a means of retaining an identity separate from that of the large masses with whom they had to share the country. The fear of being swallowed culturally, politically, and, perhaps, even physically by the autochthonous forces stimulated imitative efforts and considerably reduced the creative possibilities. The doubtful practical value of the copied ideas was compensated by the gratifications involved in the copying process. The creative spirit that could have flourished from the indigenous was atrophied by the alien. Foreign ideas acquired quick popularity and were readily accepted by the mere fact of being foreign. The ranks of those who advocated solutions based on the nature of the problems, and not on the origin of the answer, grew steadily thinner.[9]

When the intellectual movement of the mid-century got under way, the liberal and democratic ideas then so popular in European intellectual circles found immediate reception in Chile. A new political force, dogmatically committed to foreign formulas, was quickly formed. Within a very short time, the new intellectual elite, those who

9. On the Chilean tendency to imitate foreign political ideas and institutions see Enrique Tagle Rodríquez, *Liberales y Conservadores* (Santiago: Imprenta Universitaria, 1917), p. 54; Benjamín Vicuña Subercaseaux, *El socialismo revolucionario y la cuestión social en Europa y en Chile* (Santiago: Imprenta y Litografía Universo, 1908), pp. 228f.; Iñiguez, *op. cit.,* p. 141; and Benjamín Vicuña Mackenna, *Los girondinos chilenos* (Santiago: Imprenta del Comercio, 1902), p. 78. For a discussion of the same tendency in post-Napoleonic Spain see Gerald Brenan, *The Spanish Labyrinth* (Cambridge: Cambridge University Press, 1962), p. 3. Vallenilla Lanz, *op. cit.,* defines the Latin American intellectual attitude and performance as "chancletismo intelectual," a most descriptive term that cannot be translated without stripping it of its force.

fell under its influence, and the old *pipiolos* constituted an active opposition to President Montt.[10]

In 1857 the conservative group that had been the main support of the government, found itself divided. Its most intransigent wing established common cause with the liberal opposition. This extremist group, largely composed of religious zealots, accused the administration of anticlericalism and impiety. A liberal-conservative coalition was formed. President Montt retained the support of the moderate conservatives and was eventually able to add moderate liberal support as well.[11]

This arrangement of forces was indicative of even deeper changes taking place in the political structure of the country. Firmly established authoristic rule would have precluded the possibility of powerful independent parties. The increasing willingness of political factions to oppose the government reflected a decline in the nation's willful submission to an all-powerful president. But increasingly independent action did not mean that the Chilean political parties had become ideologically uniform and organizationally cohesive units. The overriding factor was the response to presidential control. Party alignment responded not so much to ideological and organizational factors as it did to the basic attitudes concerning presiden-

10. It is interesting to observe that the most influential intellectual figures in Chile during the early part of the nineteenth century were not Chileans but foreigners. This seems to indicate that during the years when the Portalian experiment (with its characteristic pragmatic orientation) was most successful, the country did not possess a native intellectual elite. It is most interesting to compare this situation with the case of Mexico after 1917 where the practical and realistic outlook that characterized the accomplishments of the revolution took place in a political situation devoid of intellectual guidance and leadership.

11. Galdames, *A History* . . . , *op. cit.,* pp. 296f.

tial rule. New political groups came into being, some accepting and others rejecting presidential supremacy. The mere existence of the choice to accept or reject the control of the executive indicated that the tide was turning against authoritism, and the attempt to institutionalize the undisputed rule of the president had fallen short of complete success.

Failure to institutionalize authoritism meant "personalization" of the presidency. The powers and prerogatives ascribed to the office came to be identified with the man in the presidential chair. The only open alternatives, under these circumstances, were legitimate personal rule (*caudillismo*), illegitimate personal rule (dictatorship), or anarchy. The dynamics of Chilean psychocultural orientation made these the only viable options.

The same dynamic principles of organization that applied to presidential rule, applied to party organization. Whether the parties remained loyal to the administration or not, their organizational foundations were similar. Those supporting the administration accepted the president as their *caudillo* and shaped their political life around him. The parties in the opposition were formed around charismatic leaders, or they were anarchical units with little effective political power. The lives of these parties, although adorned with ideological overtones, must be understood in terms of the personalities who controlled them. The basic element in the organization of party units was thus in accord with the most orthodox political tradition of the country.

Ideological commitments played only a secondary role in the internal organization and subsequent actions of the parties. The influence of foreign ideas was strongly felt in the nation's political life but not through the machinery of the parties. The political impact of these ideas was primarily felt in the psychosocial process that in turn determined party action. The intellectual elite, through books, newspapers, lectures, magazines and the like brought into the political picture a new set of symbols. In their minds, the ideas of progress and "European" were similar. The new foreign political conceptions were widely accepted, in principle, by everyone. But the intellectual commitment was unable to change the real nature of Chilean politics. The parties in favor of democracy and liberalism remained strongly attached to dictatorial functional procedures. Once again in the Chilean political arena the duality between ideals and reality started to achieve dangerous proportions. Ideological labels became obviously superficial and under these circumstances an alliance between conservatives and liberals was neither strange nor illogical.

This is not to say, of course, that ideology did not affect political action. It certainly did. In a culture predisposed to dogmatic commitments the new ideas were accepted as sacred principles. In the traditional fashion, they became goals to be achieved rather than directional principles of behavior. All parties took in the most prominent political ideals, but the degree to which these principles were allowed to influence their action was related to the type of leadership of the party in question. The parties with strong charismatic leaders paid only lip service to ideological principles. The parties with weak leadership exalted their ideological commitment to a greater degree. The former group retained a somewhat more pragmatic orientation than the latter.[12]

---

12. A similar phenomenon can be observed throughout Latin America. Parties under caudillistic rule generally appear to have a more pragmatic orientation than those ideologically committed. As a result of this, non-ideological groups, usually

The extremist political factions became increasingly antagonistic to the Montt administration. The positive accomplishments of the government, which were many and varied, did not prevent the growth of an opposition that justified its actions with grandiloquent idealistic pronouncements. The liberal opposition actively campaigned in favor of democratizing and liberalizing the country according to the latest ideas in vogue in Paris, Washington, and London. The forms of traditional authoritism proved distasteful to them. No effort was made on their part, though, to overhaul the system so that it could meet the needs of new times. Instead, they advocated its complete abolition on grounds that it was archaic and antidemocratic. In their interpretation they were directly helped by the governmental forces who, also under the influence of the intellectual groups, agreed that the alien principles had a universal value and were thus applicable to Chile. The opposition was dreaming of magical formulas that would render Chile liberal and democratic overnight. The forces in power, instead of defending the principles of government and political organization they represented, succumbed to the overpowering desire to be "European" and "progressive." They did not challenge the new concepts but, on the contrary, felt compelled to declare themselves in favor of them. Since the reality of the country rendered such principles nonoperational, those in power found themselves in need of violating in practice the ideas they adhered to in theory. Their political pragmatism was retained at the price of moral duplicity.

From 1831 to 1861 Chile progressed economically, defeated the Bolivian-Peruvian confederation, and con-

---

controlled by a charismatic personality, have had more political success than the doctrinaire groups.

solidated its territorial integrity. The reestablishment of authoritism had not been an unqualified success, but it will be very difficult to deny its links with military victories, internal progress and the stability the country enjoyed during those years. But the final years of the Montt administration were plagued with political difficulties. The authoritistic principle, under Liberal and Conservative attack, lost force. The president failed to get Antonio Varas, his close friend and political protégé, to succeed him in office. José Joaquín Pérez, a member of the National party, but one who was acceptable to the opposition, became the official candidate. Still very much responding to authoritistic tendencies, the opposition, quite aware of its weakness, was much more concerned with influencing the nomination of the official candidate than with electing its own. It was an accepted fact of Chilean political life that the official candidate would inevitably be elected.[13]

From Authoritism to Dictatorship

The second epoch of the Portalian era begins with the Pérez administration. After 1861 deep changes took place in the economic and social structure of the country. A manufacturing and commercial class emerged. The absolute social and economic political predominance of the landed aristocracy was seriously challenged, and the upcoming forces, while struggling for acceptance and power, became the ardent advocates of the new liberal ideas.[14] The spirit of the prior years was quickly changing. In the absence of any desire to build from within, the new challenges had to be met with imported formulas. The

13. On the controls over the electoral process exercised by the presidents of this period see Castedo, *op. cit.*, Vol. II, p. 1008.
14. Jobet, *Ensayo . . . , op. cit.*, p. 40.

desire to create and develop pluralistic institutions gained in strength and a break with the traditional forms became unavoidable.[15]

President Pérez soon lost the support of the National party that had elected him, and the Liberal-Conservative coalition was brought into the government. But not all the Liberals followed their party's easy march into power. The most doctrinaire and radical among them refused to support the new administration. José Joaquín Pérez was neither a charismatic nor a forceful leader, and the limitations of his appeal augmented the possibilities of political and doctrinaire opposition to his rule.

The congressional elections of 1864, produced, through the executive control of the electoral machinery, an increase in the strength of the Liberal-Conservative legislative representation. The Nationals, now in the opposition, began to actively campaign, with the help of the Radicals, for constitutional reforms that would considerably diminish the power of the president. Partially out of political rancor and rivalry, and partially out of ideological conviction, they now joined the liberal cry for reform.

The liberals in power faced a peculiar situation in which their ideological commitments collided with their political interests. Long-time champions of the need to do away with authoritistic ways, they supported the changing of the law while at the same time—admitting the need for strong rule—they adhered to the high-handed actions of the executive. Their behavior was one with long roots in the Roman-Spanish-Chilean tradition. Homage was paid to principles while actual political action was determined by the realities and needs of the country. Once in power, the liberals became a peculiar breed of night-

15. Heise, *op. cit.*, p. 57.

time advocates of pluralism and daytime supporters of presidential supremacy.

During Pérez's first term, Chile was involved in an international conflict with Spain that diverted the country's attention and imposed cooperation among the antagonistic political factions. When the conflict ended, a new outburst of political passions plagued Pérez's second term. The opposition created numerous clubs of reform in which new political ideas were expounded. Under external and internal liberal pressure the government carried out reforms in the fields of religious freedom and civil liberties. Far from being satisfied, the most militant members of the opposition saw the actions of the government as signs of weakness that called for stronger and more radical attempts. In a country with little or no tradition of political compromise, this conclusion was warranted. The government coalition steadfastly opposed the new reforms, and of all the changes propounded by the opposition only the one forbidding the immediate reelection of the president was implemented during the last five years of the Pérez administration.[16] This structural change which took the form of a constitutional amendment, was both a reflection of the declining power of the presidency and an added factor to such a decline.

Federico Errázuriz Zañartu succeeded José Joaquín Pérez in 1871. Soon after his inauguration, the country was in the middle of a bitter political struggle. The new president was an old-time liberal who was exiled to Peru for participating in the 1851 revolt. He was so well disposed toward the opposition's demands that in 1873 the governing Liberal-Conservative coalition was broken and the president formed an all-Liberal cabinet. A Liberal-

16. For a brief but learned description of the Pérez administration see Galdames, *A History . . . , op. cit.,* pp. 305ff.

Radical congressional coalition now lent its support to the government while the Conservatives were returned to the ranks of the opposition. A series of legal reforms were enacted. Freedom of the press was instituted and the power of the church curtailed. A far-reaching revision of the constitution took place in 1874. Limitations were placed on the presidential prerogative to decree a state of siege. The election of the supreme judicial body was turned over to congress. Civil liberties were guaranteed and the independence of the judiciary affirmed.[17]

The constitution was modified and new laws were enacted, but the country obstinately refused to let itself be molded by the written precepts. The liberal laws did not effect any immediate fundamental change in political attitudes or interpersonal relations. Deprived of the legal means of electoral control held by his predecessors, the president was forced to find new ways of retaining his firm grip over the elections. This concession to theoretical liberalism placed the president in an inherently dual position. The letter of the law demanded that he abstain from interfering in the electoral process while in practice he was still expected to run the electoral show. His followers as well as the country at large expected it.[18] The need for a directional force and a commanding voice was still a vital factor in Chilean politics. Devoid of legal machinery to accomplish the expected task, the executive

17. Ricardo Salas Edwards, *Balmaceda y el parlamentarismo en Chile: un estudio de psicología política chilena* (Santiago: Imprenta Universo, 1914), Vol. I, pp. 73f. For a description of the reforms enacted see Donoso, *op. cit.,* pp. 441ff.
18. *Hope* cannot be equated in this case with *expectancy.* Even the most ardent liberals who sincerely *hoped* to change the system, *expected* the president to act as the ultimate electoral force. The fact that the liberals were in power when the reforms were both approved in theory and violated in practice would lend support to this interpretation.

was forced to turn to fraud and violence. The electoral reforms failed to remove presidential influence from the Chilean elections.[19] Instead, they demanded that the president operate at the margin of the law. After 1871, the president no longer directed but forced electoral results. Acceptance of presidential control was withering away, and in the absence of allegiance, the president had to resort to trickery and violence in order to discharge the traditional functions of its office.

The personal convictions of the man in office could not alter in any meaningful way the course of events. The pressures upon the president to use naked power were irresistable. In order to rule, the chief executive had to violate the new constitutional precepts and overcome the militant antagonism of those who were either in favor of them or using them to rationalize their political position. Under these circumstances, the president was propelled into an operational vicious circle. The more force he used, the less the allegiance rendered to him; and the less his legitimacy became, the more he needed to use violence. Slowly, but steadily, the authoritistic president of the first half of the Portalian era became the political boss and dictator of the second.

When Aníbal Pinto assumed the presidency of Chile in 1876, the system of government no longer resembled that of the 1831-1861 era. What had been a respected, dignified, and powerful office was just becoming the control center of official fraud and violence. The president, who had been an esteemed moderator, evolved into a despised dictator. The decline of presidential authoritism produced an increase in the political importance of congress. Once

---

19. Castedo, *op. cit.*, Vol. III, pp. 1619 and 1626. See also Joaquín Rodríguez Bravo, *Balmaceda y el conflicto entre el congreso y el ejecutivo* (Santiago: Imprenta Gutenberg, 1921), p. 50.

the willing submission of congressmen was lost, executive control over congress depended largely on official electoral fraud and deceit. The lack of respect for the president and his rule was a potent factor in the growing congressional wish for independence and power of its own. At the same time, although the president tightly controlled the great majority of the electoral districts, there were areas where the amount of force and deception required to elect the official candidate was too demanding and the government permitted the opposition to win.[20]

The more independent and daring congress became, the tighter executive control over the elections was required if the president was to retain his commanding position.[21] The more dictatorial (illegitimate) the system turned, the larger and more militant the opposition. The weakening of presidential power was so swift, some Chilean historians are convinced that had it not been for the war of the Pacific,[22] President Prieto may never have finished his term in office.[23] The international conflict diverted the country's attention from the pressing internal crisis, and under the banner of unity and patriotism the administration in office was able to complete its term.

In 1881, the year the war with Peru ended, Domingo Santa María was inaugurated president of the republic. His candidacy was supported by the Nationals, Liberals, and Radicals, and the new chief executive was elected without any active opposition. General Manuel Baque-

---

20. Salas, *op. cit.,* Vol. I, pp. 35f.
21. *Ibid.,* Vol. I, pp. 49f.
22. This was the conflic in which Chile was engaged against Peru and Bolivia from 1879 to 1884. As a result of it Chile acquired its present northern provinces. For an account of this war see Gonzalo Bulnes, *La guerra del Pacífico* (Santiago: Editorial del Pacífico, S.A., 1955-1956).
23. Castedo, *op. cit.,* Vol. III.

dano, a well-known hero of the war, was a contender for the nomination but decided to retire from the race when he failed to gather enough support.

The military victory and territorial gains that resulted from the conflict with Peru and Bolivia did not preclude, once the war was over, the continuation of the violent internal strife. President Santa María was personally more forceful and politically more able than his predecessor, Pinto. He ruled with a strong hand and made use of skillful political manipulation. But despite his mastery of political techniques and electoral manipulative skills, he was not able to change the direction in which the nation was geared. The best he could do was maintain himself in office; he could not stop the mounting antagonism expressed toward the office itself.

Under the Santa María administration further legal liberalization took place. In 1884 laws providing for civil marriage and registry was passed, and the right of the government to arrest private persons was restricted. The following year congress was given the right to override the presidential veto when dealing with constitutional amendments, and more electoral reforms were introduced. As with the other reforms, the new measures did not bring about any appreciable change in political behavior along the lines prescribed by the new laws. If anything, the new rules forced the president to resort to more extralegal action. The more sweeping theoretical democracy was, the harsher and more dictatorial actual presidential rule became. The numerous electoral reforms enacted since 1861 did not prevent Santa María from going to all lengths to deprive his opponents of a fair chance of achieving power.[24]

Although the majority of congressmen were in fact

---

24. Galdames, *A History* . . . , *op. cit.,* pp. 339ff.

presidential appointees, congress, as an institution, sought to take advantage of the decline in executive prestige. The struggle between president and congress under Santa María gained force and bitterness.[25] It was a fight not for a greater share of power, but for total control. Theoretical adherence to pluralistic principles had not altered the monistic and absolutistic tendencies of the society and its members. Congress wanted to eliminate presidential power from the political scene. The president tried to preserve his influence over congressional elections. Corrupt practices increased rapidly under the auspices of the executive.[26] But the increase in electoral manipulation was not accompanied by a rise in congressional loyalty.[27] The waning of presidential authority had reached such a degree that those virtually appointed by the president to their congressional seats felt no marked loyalty toward his office or person. The determinant causes of the political battle taking place only indirectly related to the ideology and organization of competing factions. The real issue in question was by then the total breakdown of presidential authoritism and the reactions to it. The Chilean political scene was a contest between a dictatorial civilian president and an increasingly unmanageable congress, that, responding to the dynamics of the situation, was trying to move into the growing power vacuum.

Domingo Santa María governed Chile as an unscrupulous political boss. Under his administration, electoral dishonesty and political violence were on the increase.[28] Disregard for proper form was so marked, the

25. Heise, *op. cit.,* p. 80.
26. Agustín Edwards, *Cuatro presidentes de Chile* (Valparaíso: Sociedad, Imprenta y Litografía Universo, 1932), Vol. II, p. 268.
27. Salas, *op. cit.,* Vol. I, p. 78.
28. According to Carlos Walker Martínez, *Historia de la adminis-*

president would sometimes amuse himself, immediately after the elections had been held, by proclaiming elected for certain districts, candidates who supposedly had run for different ones.[29] By the end of Santa María's term, the last vestiges of presidential authoritism had disappeared. The system that had been so instrumental in preserving internal order and stability since 1831 was living its last moments. After half a century of marked departure from what were already characteristic Latin American patterns of political conduct and organization, Chile was well on her way to joining the ranks of her sister republics.

The Balmaceda Administration: The Final Collapse

In spite of the opposition's attempt to force the government to withdraw its candidacy, José Manuel Balmaceda was elected president in 1886. His administration succeeded in the areas of public works, education, and public finances. In spite of these accomplishments the new president was always faced with a militant and daring opposition.

---

tración Santa María, (Santiago: Imprenta del Progreso, 1888–1889), Vol. II, p. 221, the number of people injured or killed during the elections had been rising at the following rate: election of 1882, 7 injured, 2 dead; election of 1885, 165 injured, 12 dead; election of 1886, an incomplete account showed 160 injured, 46 dead. Although Walker Martínez was an active member of the opposition to President Santa María, and, therefore, his figures may not be completely reliable, the increase in violence at election time is not denied by any Chilean historian. The same author also offers a very partial but nonetheless interesting description of the techniques employed by the government's armed groups. For an analysis of the general orientation of the Santa María administration see Humberto Alegría Reyes, Orientación política de la administración de Santa María (Santiago, 1946).

29. Rodríguez Bravo, Balmaceda y . . . , op. cit., p. 35.

Balmaceda, following in the footsteps of his immediate predecessors, tried to consolidate his position by keeping tight control over the electoral machinery. Very soon, all the seats in congress, with the exception of the ten won by the Conservatives, were filled with Balmaceda's personal choices, but as had been the case with the previous administrations, congressional loyalty still proved quite evasive.[30] Realizing this, the president attempted to alleviate the executive-legislative tension by appeasing his opponents. Out of thirteen ministerial crises in the government, seven were solved in cooperation with the opposition.[31] But the efforts of the president were destined to fail. The sincerity of his overture seems to have been doubtful in the light of subsequent events, but even if his efforts were sincere, grounds for a working peace between the contending factions no longer existed. Furthermore, the president's courting of his enemies was—within the Chilean context—an unmistakable sign of weakness which increased the hopes of congress and intensified the legislative quest for control.[32]

Unable to subdue congress, Balmaceda's problems rapidly increased. The legislators now showed open signs

---

30. *Ibid.,* p. 159.
31. Heise, *op. cit.,* p. 73. See also the speech delivered by Balmaceda on January 1, 1890 that is reproduced in Alfredo Edwards Barros, *Balmaceda, su vida y actuación como primer mandatario hasta el 1o. de enero de 1891* (Santiago: Editorial "Antares," 1936), p. 47.
32. Alex Inkeles, "The Totalitarian Mystique: Some Impressions of the Dynamics of Totalitarian Society," in Carl J. Friedrich (ed.), *Totalitarianism: Proceedings of a Conference held at the American Academy of Arts and Science.* (Cambridge: Harvard University Press, 1954), pp. 87ff., deals with some of the implications of the inability to share power on the part of the leaders of certain societies. Much of Inkele's analysis could be useful in studying the characteristics of Chilean political development.

of defiance in the face of executive pressure. The president, unable to control those same legislators he had helped gain office, knew congress was trying to destroy his office as a politically powerful institution.[33] Aware that his only two alternatives were to strengthen his hold or to surrender completely, he chose to fight.[34]

The Conservative pro-clerical group was the most vocal and militant faction in the opposition to President Balmaceda. In their fight against the government, they became the most resolute defendants of constitutional democratic principles and the most ardent enemies of presidential supremacy. That the Conservatives had so radically changed their political position in just a few years was indicative of the limited influence of party philosophy over the actual determination of political actions. The zealous defenders of religious intolerance and clerical privileges were now fighting, in the name of freedom and democracy, against the more open-minded Liberals who supported presidential dictatorship.

The emergence of a militant proletarian class and the devaluation of paper money with its inflationary consequences, further complicated the feeble existence of the government. The new problems and the inability of the president to cope with them highlighted the weakness of the system. Remedy was once more sought in liberal reforms now violated almost as soon as they were enacted. Around 1861 authoritism had given way to dictatorship. Chaos was setting in.

The majority of the nation's population remained aloof from political participation. The battle for power

33. See the speech of Balmaceda reproduced in Edwards Barros, *op. cit.,* pp. 46f.
34. Nevin O. Winter, *Chile and her People of Today* (Boston: L. C. Pace and Co., 1922), pp. 342f.

was circumscribed to the small number of groups and individuals who constituted the national political elite. The struggle took place among the small number of people who controlled the social, economic, intellectual, and military life of Chile. This lack of widespread national concern with politics precluded any serious attempt on the part of either congress or the president to enlist active popular support under their respective banners.[35]

A climax in executive-legislative tension was reached in late 1890 when congress turned down the administration's appropriation bill for the new fiscal year. The refusal of congress to pass on the appropriation laws or to vote supplies for the armed forces was a direct attack on the president. Confronted with an open challenge to his rule, Balmaceda got ready to counter-attack. On January 1, 1891, the president promulgated, by executive decree, the budget of the previous year. In the manifesto to the nation that followed his action he tried to justify his conduct on legal and constitutional grounds.

Congress interpreted the executive's action as an actual coup d'etat. Balmaceda was immediately accused of having violated the constitution and of illegal seizure of power.[36] The legislators reacted promptly and drastically—the majority of them signed a document deposing the president. Through their action, congress was now in formal revolt against the president. On January 7, the

---

35. Chilean historians agree that lack of popular participation in politics was characteristic of this time. On this subject see Heise, *op. cit.*, p. 109; and Castedo, *op. cit.*, Vol. III, p. 1737. For a Marxist interpretation of this struggle see Jobet, *op. cit.*; and for a non-Marxist account see Alberto Edwards, *La fronda . . . , op. cit.*, pp. 151ff.

36. Antonio Iñiguez Vicuña, *El golpe de estado i la revolución: primero i siete de enero de 1891* (Santiago: Imprenta "Victoria," 1891), p. 9.

ships of the fleet stationed at Valparaíso started to move northward carrying the leaders of the congressional movement. The country was once more involved in a civil war. A people whose cultural, psychological and political make-up made them responsive to authoritistic symbols and commands would most certainly tend toward anarchical behavior if the restraints to which they were prone to respond were removed without adequate provision for effective substitutes.

The increasing unrest felt by the country was clearly reflected in the attitude of the military. Once its loyalty to the executive started to wane, the military showed increasing willingness to intervene in politics. In the void created by the decline of authoritism, the armed forces saw a place for themselves.[37] By the time the insurrection erupted, President Balmaceda was unable to muster the kind of military support enjoyed by his predecessors during the first half of the Portalian era. Military unrest mounted during the last few years when both president and congress openly coveted its support, and military leaders were active in the political feud between Balmaceda and the legislature.[38] When war broke out, the

---

37. The attempt to explain Latin American militarism in terms of personal ambitions or class consciousness is only partially satisfactory. The existence of a desire—or orientation—for forceful rule, places the military *ipso facto* in a prominent political position. When the civilian government is not able to provide the expected rule, the most probable alternatives are chaos or military takeover. It goes without saying, that individual military leaders and special socioeconomic interests are, under such circumstances, in a privileged position to further their interests at the expense of the country at large.

38. For a description of the political activities of the members of the armed forces during the Balmaceda administration see Rodríguez Bravo, *Balmaceda y . . . , op. cit.,* p. 181. On the same subject see also Edwards Barros, *op. cit.,* pp. 41ff.

military, in a politically strategic position, carefully chose sides.

One of the most important characteristics of presidential authoritism in Chile is that it kept political power in the hands of civilians. This, of course, was also one of the main features of Spanish colonial authoritism. The reasons for it are quite clear. Under the authoritistic system, the degree of allegiance elicited from the politically influencial forces, including the military, was such that it acted as a psychological impediment, in most cases, to revolt and military takeover. This psychological impediment functioned not only as a vague abstraction but also as a meaningful threat. Loyalty to the president meant, among other things, there were forces willing to battle in his behalf. This was an added consideration in the mind of any potentially mutinous soldier.

The insurrection against Balmaceda followed an uncertain course until the month of August when the battles of Concón and Placilla signaled the total defeat of the loyal troops. During the seven months of the revolt, the president tried in vain to cling to his power. He called a constitutional convention into session with the intention of strengthening his legal position.[39] But time had run out. In the declining process and eventual breakdown of presidential authoritism and dictatorship, José Manuel

---

39. Although elections for the convention were held, the convention never met. Balmaceda's Minister of Interior, Julio Bañados in his *La reforma constitucional y la administración Balmaceda* (Santiago: Imprenta Nacional, 1891) gives a detailed account of the constitutional changes Balmaceda considered necessary. The same author in his *Balmaceda: su gobierno y la revolución de 1891* (Paris: Librería de Garnier Hermanos, 1894) describes and evaluates the civil war from a pro-Balmaceda point of view.

Balmaceda had merely been the star performer of the final act.

The Balance Sheet

In examining the major political changes affecting Chile from 1831 to 1891, the importance of properly evaluating the relationship between law and reality during this era is evident. The long series of legal reforms begun in mid-century and carried through to the administration of Balmaceda, altered the correspondence between actual circumstances and legal forms that resulted from the Portalian effort. The adoption of non-Chilean principles of government upset the balance between the legal and real constitutions. In the light of these circumstances, one may be led to the fallacious conclusion that the unreality of the law was the chief factor responsible for the political events besetting the nation. Such an inference would be unwarranted. It would be safer to assume that although such unrealistic law affected subsequent conduct and attitudes, the true etiologic factors in Chilean political behavior rested in more subtle psychological and cultural traditions and inclinations. The unreal character of the law was but one of its manifestations.

The discussion of Chile's experimentation with authoritistic rule gains importance when the accomplishments of the country after 1831 are taken into account. Under presidential authoritism Chile advanced economically and became a power in the area. Two wars were successfully fought and new lands were added to the national territory. It would be difficult not to agree that such progress was probably related to the internal order and stability. The basis for these gains were laid during the first thirty years of the Portalian era, and the decline of authoritism was accompanied by a general decay that permeated most aspects of the nation's collective life. Any comparison of Chile with the rest of the Latin American republics during this period would bring light upon the accomplishments of authoritism. Whereas Chile attained during this period a semblance of order and organization with concomitant social and economic development, the rest of Latin America was immersed in total political chaos. The other countries appeared to have been caught between unwillingness to follow known political formulas and inability to implement new ones.

The experiment with republican authoritism, and the nature of the results, clearly revealed the character of some of the fundamental political problems facing the Chileans.

The necessity to face and take reality into account—even if the final intention were to transform this same reality—in order to devise reliable political institutions and procedures, became manifest. It became equally evident that intellectualism and wishful thinking could not provide solid grounds on which to organize the nation. If the country were to attain stability and progress, escapism could not take the place of honest evaluation and firm realistic action.

VI.

The Failure of the Parliamentary Attempt

The civil war of 1891 ended with the victory of the congressional forces over the president.[1] This event signaled a change in the country's political structure. It was not only a government that had collapsed, but an entire system.[2] Executive predominance was abruptly ended, and although the 1833 constitution was retained, it was so modified that it now read as a different document.[3]

As soon as the new forces took charge of the government, they began to put into effect the political principles and ideas they had advocated in their struggle against the president. A municipal law was enacted with the intention of decentralizing governmental functions which

1. For a chronological description of this armed conflict see Antonio Aguirre Perry, *Impresiones de campaña* (Santiago: Imprenta Albión, 1892). For a somewhat different account see Carlos Baeza Yávar, *Páginas de sangre de la revolución de 1891* (Buenos Aires: Imprenta de Obras de J. A. Berra, 1894).
2. Galdames, *A History...*, *op. cit.*, pp. 361f.
3. *Ibid.*, pp. 361ff.

had been in the hands of the executive. The municipalities were granted broad powers in the areas of health, education, industrial development, and police. They were also assigned important electoral functions aimed at destroying the past presidential control over the apparatus. Furthermore, all legislative offices were closed to anyone on the public payroll. This so-called "Law of Parliamentary Incompatibility," was intended to prevent executive pressure over the legislature.[4]

The new leaders showed no interest in bringing about a balance of power between the executive and legislative branches. They were interested in establishing legislative supremacy. Although their actual concept of authority and power, as exemplified in their way of handling the executive office,[5] did not lose its monistic and absolutistic overtones,[6] the fact that congress was a collective entity allowed them to rationalize the new arrangement in terms of pluralistic and non-absolutistic theories of government. The supremacy of congress was thus instituted in the name of freedom and democracy.[7]

---

4. *Ibid.*, pp. 362f.
5. On the relations between congress and the executive during these years see Arturo Alessandri, *Chile y su historia* (Santiago: Editorial Orbe, 1945), Vol. II, p. 326; J. Valdés Cange, *Sinceridad i Chile interno en 1910* (Santigo: Imprenta Universitaria, 1910), pp. 45f.; and Moisés Poblete Troncoso, *El balance de nuestro régimen parlamentario* (Santiago: Talleres de "Numen," 1920), pp. 15f.
6. For an interesting analysis of the Chilean concept of authority see Edwards Vives, *La fronda . . .*, *op. cit.*, pp. 171ff. On the same subject see Roberto Espinoza, *La evolución democrática* (Santiago: Editores Hume y Walker, 1918), p. 325.
7. Galdames, *A History . . .*, *op. cit.*, p. 363, believes that the change from presidential omnipotence to congressional omnipotence did not bring about any fundamental alteration in the political structure of the country. Such a view, even if incorrect, would tend to support my assertion that no evidence is

The country was now caught in an inescapable dilemma. It had been provided with a system of government lacking an adequate operational basis. Congressional supremacy was really an empty term. Such supremacy had a negative effect. It limited the executive's sphere of action, but there was no apparent way of giving it a positive and effective administrative or political connotation. Congress could stop the president from ruling but it could not rule itself. On the one hand, the pluralistic intra-congressional structure was out of tune with Chilean political culture;[8] and on the other, the collective character of the congressional bodies made its development along authoritistic lines quite improbable. Under these circumstances, congressional control could not even be transformed into effective dictatorial rule. Aside from making the task of the president meaningless and often embarrassing, there was little else congress could do to attain effective rule.

Needless to say, this state of affairs was welcomed by the economic elite of the country, especially the landed gentry. They gained easy control of the recently localized electoral system and used this control to elect themselves or their representatives to congress as a guarantee that no effective measure against their interests would be taken. It is obvious that the landed aristocracy had seen in the preservation of executive predominance a threat, real or potential, to their interests. The ability of the presidential office to communicate with the country at large, and

---

to be found of changes in the basic Chilean attitudes toward political authority and power.

8. Edwards Vives, *La fronda ...*, *op. cit.*, pp. 171ff., deals with this phenomenon in terms of "The Chilean tendency to accept a master." On the same subject see also Oscar Bermúdez Miral, *El drama político de Chile* (Santiago: Editorial Tegualda, 1947), p. 10.

represent the interests of classes other than their own, must have been pesent in the minds of the conservative landowners who joined the 1891 revolt.[9] In this respect, it is necessary to keep in mind that within the Chilean political context more effective representation was possible through the executive than through the legislative. It would be quite misleading to believe that a direct relationship between effective national representation and the widening of legislative prerogatives was forthcoming. The representative quality of the executive office goes deep into the Spanish-Chilean past and psyche, and had been formalized in the moderating function ascribed to monarchs and presidents.

Parliamentary Anarchy

Six different administrations participated in the parliamentary experiment before the system collapsed: Jorge Montt, the military leader of the 1891 revolt against Balmaceda, from 1891 to 1896; Federico Errázuriz Echaurren from 1896 to 1901;[10] Germán Riesco, from 1901 to 1906;[11] Pedro Montt, from 1906 to 1910.[12] Montt died while he

---

9. Edwards Vives, *La fronda . . .* , *op. cit.,* pp. 171ff., links the parliamentary regime in Chile to the socio-economic elite of the country. On the political role of the Chilean aristocracy during this epoch see also Heise, *op. cit.,* p. 76; and, Wilhem Mann, *Chile luchando por nuevas formas de vida* (Santiago: Prensas de la Editorial Ercilla, 1935–1936), Vol. I, p. 68.

10. For a detailed analysis of the Errázuriz Echaurren administration see Jaime Eyzaguirre, *Chile durante el gobierno de Errázuriz Echaurren, 1896–1906* (Santiago: Empresa Editoria Zig-Zag, S.A., 1957).

11. For an account of the Riesco administration see Germán Riesco, *Presidencia de Riesco, 1901–1906* (Santiago: Editorial Nascimento, 1950).

12. A general idea of how the parliamentary system worked is provided by Galdames, *A history . . . . op. cit.,* p. 367, in his analysis of the Montt administration.

held office and was replaced by his vice-president, Elías Fernández Albano, who also died in office, and was succeeded by Emiliano Figueroa. Ramón Barros Luco was elected in 1910, and Juan Luis Sanfuentes in 1915. During these administrations the subordination of the executive to congress did not diminish,[13] nor did congress' ability to rule improve. The political life of the nation came to a standstill. Congress failed to deal with the pressing problems of the country, and at the same time it forestalled executive initiative.[14]

Governmental ineffectiveness was increased by the constant intervention of congress in all aspects of executive action. The members of the legislature even intervened in minor details of provincial administration. Congress was ruled by occasional combinations of parties, usually formed to overthrow a given ministerial cabinet but totally unable to develop and carry through a program of government.[15] Chile was, in fact, without a government. The institutional structure existed, but did not function. The parliamentary experiment degenerated into governmental anarchy.

As early as 1909, José A. Alfonso was labeling the parliamentary system as anarchical.[16] A later analyst explains the ineffectiveness of the government in terms of ministerial weakness. According to him, the position of

---

13. Alessandri, *op. cit.*, Vol.I, p. 175.
14. Carlos Pinto Durán, *La revolución chilena* (Santiago: Imprenta Valiente y Cía., 1925), p. 85; Carlos Keller, *Un país al garete: contribución a la sismología social de Chile* (Santiago: Editorial Nascimento, 1932); and Raúl Marín, *La caída de un régimen* (Santiago: Imprenta Universtaria, 1933), p. 10.
15. Heise, *op. cit.*, p. 76; and J. T. Ramírez, *Historia de Chile* (Santiago: n.d.), p. 284.
16. *El parlamentarismo i la reforma política en Chile* (Santiago: Cabeza y Cía., Impresores, 1909), p. 8.

the cabinet members, and thus of the executive as a whole, became so weak that the ministers had to ask as favors for the power to do things they would have been entitled to do under any other system of government.[17]

Under the tutelage of congress, Chile came to enjoy, in theory, an electoral system that would provoke the envy of any democratic nation.[18] In practice, however, electoral corruption increased.[19] Executive control of congressional elections was replaced by the buying of votes and other forms of electoral fraud. Plutocratic interests took over the electoral process, and consolidated their control of congress.[20] The Chilean aristocracy became once again the political master of the nation. But its grip was not a firm one.[21]

By 1920 the country was feeling the consequences of the lack of effective government. Some of the problems withered away, but others stubbornly refused to disappear. The country was undergoing social and economic changes that demanded official attention and action. Parliamentary anarchy was unable to solve them. The weakness of the system, so obvious since its inception, became intolerable. Senator Arturo Alessandri, a presidential candidate, took full advantage of the social and political contest and won an easy victory on a reform platform.[22]

---

17. Poblete, *op. cit.,* p. 32.
18. Salas *op. cit., Vol. I,* p. 163.
19. For a general discussion of some of the Chilean electoral vices see Ricardo Cruz Coke, *Geografía electoral de Chile* (Santiago: Editorial del Pacífico, S.A., 1952), pp. 55f.
20. Ricardo Donoso, *Alessandri, agitador y demoledor: cincuenta años de historia política de Chile* (México City: Fondo de Cultura Económica, 1952–1954), Vol. I, p. 178.
21. Edwards Vives, *La fronda . . . , op. cit.,* pp. 177f.; and Alfonso, *op. cit.,* pp. 13ff.
22. Donoso, *Alessandri . . . , op. cit.,* Vol. I, pp. 240f. For an interpretation of the social changes taking place in the country dur-

Once elected, Alessandri was faced with a difficult political situation. The majority of the House of Deputies was in favor of his plan of reforms but the majority of the Senate was against it. Under the parliamentary system the cabinet had to keep the confidence of both houses, so the President was unable to implement his program of government. His ministers did not last long, some of them a few weeks, others a few months. Not only did they encounter opposition in the Senate, but sometimes among the better disposed deputies as well.[23] The political crisis in the country and the importance of the issues at stake, gave rise to an active antagonism between the two congressional chambers that resulted in even greater ineffectiveness and inaction. Finally, after much effort, the president was able to get part of his reform program approved by congress.[24] But Alessandri was not satisfied with this partial accomplishment and he strongly advocated the introduction of new and more radical economic and social reforms. His attempts in this direction were blocked by the Senate opposition.

The Downfall of Congressional Rule

The political situation of the country, as well as the urgent need for economic and social reforms, led the president and his associates to believe that some urgent reforms were needed in the political structure. Their immediate concern was depriving the Senate of its power to block executive action. When the congressional election of 1924 approached, Alessandri campaigned vigorously. He and his political associates asked the electorate to

---

ing these years see Edwards Vives, *La fronda . . . , op. cit.,* pp. 183ff.

23. Galdames, *A History . . . , op. cit.,* pp. 371f.

24. Donoso, *Alessandri . . . , op. cit.,* Vol. I, pp. 277ff.

support those candidates who were in favor of the President's program of reforms.[25]

The congressional elections resulted in a victory for the political alliance backing Alessandri and his program. The new congress convened in June 1924 but was unable to accomplish any work. From June until September it failed to deal with any of the urgent problems awaiting solution. Then in September, instead of dealing with any of the pending legislation, it simply began to deal with a project of law providing for parliamentary compensation. In the explosive climate of those days this action was a bombshell.

The congressional action was unconstitutional since the constitution clearly specified that no renumeration was to be paid to the members of the legislature. But public wrath was provoked perhaps even more by the preference given to this issue over so many other urgent problems facing congress. Governmental anarchy reached a new climax and, as could have been expected, the military decided to take matters into their own hands. Army officers stationed in Santiago undertook to represent public sentiment and stop the compensation act from being carried out. A military committee was organized, and, with the consent of the Inspector-in-Chief of the army, asked the president to veto the law and recommend action on other matters of national concern.[26] On the fifth of September they moved to take over the government and three days later Alessandri resigned.[27]

Military intervention in politics was not a new phe-

---

25. *Ibid.,* Vol. I,pp. 350ff.
26. Galdames, *A History . . . , op. cit.,* p. 374.
27. For a description of the military coup that overthrew Alessandri see Juan A. Bennett, *La revolución del cinco de septiembre de 1924* (Santiago: Editores Balcells and Cía., n.d.).

nomenon in Chilean history. As discussed in the preceding chapter, the political activities of the military increased and became more effective after the deterioration of authoritistic rule. Immediately prior to and after the 1891 civil war, military interest in politics was at a peak.[28] Signs of discontent among the men in uniform were quite patent during the years of congressional rule. In 1912 a military league tried openly to influence politics,[29] and in 1919, the idea of open intervention in governmental affairs was frankly discussed by military men who were concerned with the popular demonstrations of November 1918.[30]

The failure of congressional rule set the stage for the military takeover. The political behavior of the military cannot be explained in terms of personal ambitions. Rather, military action was prompted by the collapse of civilian government. Military men are always, by the nature of their profession, in an exceptional political position—they monopolize the means of coercion. The only way to keep them under civilian control for any prolonged period of time is by gaining their psychological allegiance to such rule. As part of the nation, they respond to the same cultural tendencies present in everybody else. Within the Chilean context, military allegiance could be gained only by an idealistic and monistic symbol of authority. The system of congressional supremacy had been a far cry from this.

---

28. For a comment on military political activities after 1891 see Edwards Barros, *op. cit.,* p. 44.
29. Donoso, *Alessandri . . . , op. cit.,* Vol. I, p. 227.
30. Pinto, *op. cit.,* p. 55. For a detailed account of this military conspiracy see Donoso, *Alessandri . . . , op. cit.,* Vol. I, pp. 227ff. For a general account of military activities and ideas during this whole period see Agustín Castelblanco y Emilio Courbet, "El movimiento militar chileno," in *Revista Nosotros,* year XVII, (December 1924), number 187.

General Altamirano took over the government from Alessandri, and remained in power until January 23, 1925, when he was replaced by a military junta. The new military government enacted a long series of decree-laws, advocated the need for a new constitution, and then recalled Alessandri from exile to the presidential chair. Alessandri reassumed power in March 1925.[31] But his return could not solve, by itself, the political crisis. The simple reestablishment of civilian rule was not enough. Even if the president's recall testified to the desire, on the part of the military leaders, to preserve the constitutional structure, the type of government he represented was dead. In all honesty, the military cannot be blamed for the destruction of the system. They merely were removing its corpse.

The Constitution of 1925

The experience of his earlier years in office taught Arturo Alessandri the need for a strong executive. He was aware that the business of government could not properly be carried out in Chile otherwise. As soon as he was back in office he began to work for the creation of constitutional devices that would enhance the authority and powers of the presidency. A consultative commission was organized, and in July of 1925 it issued a report on needed constitutional reforms. Its recommendations were sanctioned by a public plebiscite.[32]

What began as a reform action ended as a new political constitution.[33] The Senate and Chamber of Deputies

---

31. Donoso, *Alessandri . . . , op. cit.*, Vol. I, pp. 373ff.
32. Galdames, *A History . . . , op. cit.*, p. 376.
33. For analysis of this constitution see José Guillermo Guerra, *La constitución de 1925* (Santiago: Establecimientos Gráficos "Balcells" y Cía., 1929); and Julio Heise González, *La constitución de 1925 y las nuevas tendencias politico-sociales* (Santiago: Editorial Universitaria, 1951).

were deprived of the power to depose ministers of the cabinet. The presidential term of office was increased to six years with the president elected by direct vote. The president was constitutionally recognized as the center of the political system, and congress was relegated to a secondary position.[34] Supremacy of the executive was so clearly recognized in the new document, it became obvious its objective was not to establish a balance of power, but to provide for executive predominance.[35]

The Constitution of 1925 was a response to the realization, on the part of the country's political leaders, that only a monistic structure would render the government operational. The preceding political chaos brought this point home, and the necessity to reestablish some continuity with the past was openly acknowledged.[36] The new constitution responded to a search for a concept of government that would be culturally acceptable to the Chileans. This is not to say that the new document was completely oriented in the direction of executive absolutism. The constitution called for a quasi-pluralistic system in which the president was given pedominance within certain limits. Article 72 stated the scope of the executive's special functions: it included the power to enact decrees and declare a state of siege. Two conflicting tendencies were present in the constitution—idealistic pluralism and realistic monism. They symbolized the hopes for the future and the acknowledgement of the past. Although the constitution meant an explicit acceptance of the cultural inclination toward monistic rule, it was a qualified acceptance tempered by an intellectual commitment to a different form of government.

---

34. Galdames, *A History . . .* , p. 376.
35. Heise, *op. cit.,* pp. 96f.
36. Galdames, *A History . . . , op. cit.,* p. 376.

The failure of the congressional system has sometimes been blamed on the lack of organization and internal cohesion of the political parties.[37] But the weakness of the Chilean political parties was in itself the result of the same forces militant against pluralism. Obviously, lack of forceful and well-disciplined political parties contributed to the overall anarchical situation, but it was far from being its causative agent. Such a superficial explanation springs from the tendency to explain political events in terms of other political events, ignoring the underlaying cultural and psychological factors. Very much the same tendency is expressed when the collapse of the parliamentary system is ascribed to its inability to deal with the mounting social and labor unrest. The system's inability to incorporate the new political forces was a symptom rather than the cause of the illness. Flexibility—the capacity to innovate and make changes—can only be a property of a secure political structure. A truly stable government adjusts itself to new situations, but a basically unstable one sees in any possible alteration of the status quo a threat to its existence.

One of the most important lessons to be learned from the years of congressional rule was that a system lacking deep roots in the nation was in no position to handle rapidly changing situations. The growing political aspirations of the middle class, the increasing unrest in the labor force, and the collapse of the nitrate boom were but three aspects of Chilean life that demanded official attention and initiative. One of the most prominent accomplishments of nineteenth-century authoritism in Chile was its ability to provide a basis for social and economic develop-

---

37. Alejandro Silva Bascuñán, *Tratado de derecho constitucional* (Santiago: Editorial Jurídica de Chile, 1963), Vol. I, p. 498; and Vol. II, pp. 45f.

ment. On the other hand congressional rule failed to integrate the middle class into the governmental structure, and this rising ambitious political force was antagonized. Inability to deal properly with the mounting economic and labor problems also helped to demonstrate the uselessness of congressional government.

One of authoritism's salient points was its integrative quality—its ability to make room within the political structure for emerging forces. Without such a capability the system could not be stable. Legal continuity and political order could not flourish if opportunity to participate were denied to the forces that through their social and economic positions were becoming politically interested and militant. Stability, therefore, was intimately related to participation.

The Years of Confusion

The new constitution was an attempt to bring peace and order by means of presidential supremacy. The constitution provided, perhaps, sufficient legal grounds for the restoration of stable and orderly government under civilian control, but the new document could not, by itself, accomplish this task. The constitutional structure was modified, but the political reality remained unaltered. The elimination of political chaos required more than beautifully written words.

In October, 1925, Arturo Alessandri was forced to resign the presidency of Chile for the second time. His Secretary of War, Colonel Carlos Ibáñez, became the actual ruler of the country. In 1927 a civilian, Emiliano Figueroa, was elected president. Before the year was over he resigned his office, clearing the way for Carlos Ibáñez, who was elected without opposition. Ibáñez ruled Chile until he was forced out of office on July 26, 1931. Although the absolute ruler of the country for a few years, Ibáñez was unable to institutionalize presidential supremacy.[38] His rule was essentially dictatorial—illegitimate in Chilean terms—and he appears to have lacked then the necessary charisma for qualifying as caudillistic.

In the three months following Ibáñez's resignation, Chile had three different presidents: Pedro Opazo Letelier, Juan Esteban Montero, and Manuel Trucco. In October 1931 Montero was officially elected president. He assumed power on December 4, 1931, and was deposed exactly six months later by a military junta[39] that immediately proclaimed the *Socialist Republic of Chile*.[40] After twelve days of precarious existence, the Socialist Republic disappeared, giving way to the dictatorship of Carlos Dávila. On September 13, a military movement forced Dávila out of office. More military convulsions followed until October 2, 1932, when the president of the Supreme Court was asked to take over the functions of chief executive. He immediately called for presidential and congressional elections. Arturo Alessandri was once more elected president of Chile.

Summary

For over seven years Chile suffered the chaotic aftermath of the congressional debacle. The military found itself propelled into the center of the political arena. Military leaders such as Ibáñez and Marmeduque Grove tried to fill the political vacuum with their personal

---

38. Bermúdez Miral, *op. cit.,* p. 21.
39. For an account of this development see Guillermo Bravo, *4 de junio: el festín de los audaces* (Santiago: Empresa Letras, n.d.).
40. For a good description of this "socialist experiment" see Donoso, *Alessandri . . . , op. cit.,* Vol. II, pp. 104ff.

leadership, but they were unsuccessful. Ibáñez held power for some time, but he could not gain national allegiance to his person or his rule. As long as the government was viewed as illegitimate, it was unstable. Theoretical adherence to the letter of the constitution did not operate as an automatic legitimizing device. The traditionally unreal interpretation of the law made the written constitution quite inoperative by itself. Its clauses providing for a certain degree of executive supremacy could only serve as rationalizing elements. They could not create presidential predominance. They merely recognized the need for such a rule. Executive leadership had to exist in reality before it could be legally justified. For seven years it did not exist in a form acceptable to the Chileans, but the reelection of Alessandri marked a turning point in the country's political life.

VII.

The Reestablishment of Presidential Authoritism

During the second administration of Arturo Alessandri the president once more became the undisputed ruler of the nation. Without vacilation, the newly elected chief executive started to strengthen the position of his office. Despite congressional censure his ministers were to stay in office as long as they retained the president's confidence. By the force of his personality Arturo Alessandri began to create, in practice, executive hegemony.[1] The presidency, after forty-one years of anarchy and disorder, became once more the accepted center of the country's political activities. Under Alessandri Chile began to find its way back to stability and legal continuity. Military intervention faded away.

---

1. Donoso, *Alessandri . . . , op. cit.,* Vol. II, pp. 120ff., describes in detail the ways and means used by Alessandri to establish his undisputed authority; see also Galdames, *A History . . . , op. cit.,* pp. 394f.

It is almost impossible to assert with clarity the degree to which different elements contributed to the new situation. Cultural forces encouraged the recreation of presidential supremacy and tended, of course, to its institutionalization. The personality of Arturo Alessandri was also well suited for the occasion.[2] He possessed charismatic qualities that evoked loyalty and allegiance. His rule could then be easily interpreted as legitimate in a psychological and cultural sense. Furthermore, the legitimacy produced by allegiance to him was projected over the constitutional structure that legally justified his regime. In other words, allegiance to Alessandri's rule made operational, for the first time, the 1925 constitution.

To believe that the constitution legitimized Alessandri's rule rather than the other way around, is putting the cart before the horse. This could have been the case, but in reality it was not. Even if it is granted that rational commitments might create or affect human behavior, it would be most unwarranted to assume that loyalty to an intellectually derived goal could supersede deeply seated cultural and psychological factors. The symbolic appeal of forceful presidential leadership was far more powerful than any expressed desire to conform to a given set of constitutional prescriptions.

Alessandri's rule had strong caudillistic elements, but also lent itself to institutionalization. It is in reference to the depersonalization of presidential supremacy that the constitutional structure was relevant. Once presidential control existed, prescribed sets of rules could, if other factors were also favorable, provide an acceptable mechanism for its preservation. How much the constitutional

2. For an antagonistic but, nevertheless, informative analysis of Alessandri's character and leadership see Donoso, *Alessandri ...*, *op. cit.*

ritual of formalization could contribute to this is difficult to determine. It would be safe to suppose it could not exceed the system's capacity to produce substantive allegiance. That is, the constitution could only be an auxiliary tool.

Arturo Alessandri was no longer the radical of the 1920's. His 1932–1938 regime was socially and economically conservative and he encountered the active opposition of the leftist groups. This conservatism is not to be confused with the politically stagnant situation that existed under congressional government. Those opposed to the policies of the government were allowed to participate in political affairs. They were not invited to join the government, but they were given a meaningful opportunity to capture the seats of power. They could oppose the president, or his policies, but were not inclined to destroy the system. It is interesting to notice how the president could evade some of the criticism that would have been, under different circumstances, directed at him. Gustavo Ross, the president's right arm in financial affairs, became the opposition's scapegoat. He was the object of much hatred and ill will for carrying out policies that were, in any final analysis, the responsibility of the chief executive.

The Popular Front and the Radical Governments

The presidential elections of 1938 ended with the victory of Pedro Aguirre Cerda over Gustavo Ross. The forces responsible for his election were a conglomeration of middle class and labor groups.[3] Alessandri's institution-

---

3. For a historical interpretation of the Chilean labor movement see Tulio Lagos Valenzuela, *Bosquejo histórico del movimiento obrero en Chile* (Santiago: Imprenta El Esfuerzo, 1941). On the same subject see Moisés Poblete Troncoso, *El movimiento de asociación profesional obrera en Chile* (México City: Fondo de Cultura Económica, 1945).

alization of presidential authoritism had been successful enough to permit the transfer of the government away from interest groups that held power almost without interruption since 1891. It is true that Aguirre Cerda himself was closer to the upper than to the middle classes and control of congress was kept by the representatives of the wealthy groups—the Liberal and the Conservative parties. Nevertheless, the fact that a new socioeconomic force was now sharing political power was inescapable. Such a transition had taken place peacefully under a system that provided legitimacy and continuity.

The Popular Front responsible for Aguirre Cerda's election was shortlived. Actually constituted under Communist initiative in 1936, it ran candidates for the first time in the congressional elections of 1937, but after its great triumph of 1938 it began to disintegrate. The Communists never participated in the government, and they claimed their real contribution could only be made as detached critics. The Socialists withdrew from the alliance in 1940, and by 1941 the Popular Front had ceased to exist.[4] The president was left to rule with the support of his party—the Radical Party—and other splinter leftist groups.[5]

Aguirre Cerda resigned from the presidency in November 1941 and died shortly afterwards. After a vigorous campaign the Radicals, with the assistance of a group of small parties, were again victorious. Juan Antonio Ríos

---

4. For an analysis of the Front see John R. Stevenson, *The Chilean Popular Front* (Philadelphia: University of Pennsylvania Press, 1942). For a shorter analysis and evaluation see Ernst Halperin, *Nationalism and Communism in Chile* (Cambridge, Massachusetts: The M.I.T. Press, 1965).

5. On the relationship between the Radical Party and the Popular Front see Alfredo G. Bravo, *El Partido Radical y el Frente Popular* (Santiago, 1938).

became president of Chile. Under the Ríos administration, in 1943, some constitutional changes were introduced that tended to increase the prerogatives of the chief executive. Presidential initiative was expanded and his constitutional position strengthened.[6] In general, however, this administration was as much concerned with international issues as with domestic ones. Ríos, who died in office in 1946, was a moderate president, and under his regime no drastic social or economic changes took place. Ríos' death made a presidential election necessary, and Gabriel González Videla, a Radical candidate supported by a coalition of center and left parties that included the Communists, came out first in the electoral contest among the four competitors, but failed to secure the required fifty-one percent majority. With the added support of the Liberal party his election was secured in congress, and González Videla assumed power with a cabinet formed by Liberals and Communists as well as Radicals.

The Communist ministers resigned after five months in office and the Liberals followed in 1947. In 1948 the Communist party was outlawed and its cadres put in prison until the second half of 1949, when the party, although still legally banned, began to function as a political entity again. Inter- and intra-party struggle seems to have been the main political distinction of González Videla's six-year rule. Coalitions were made and unmade and new parties created at a mercurial rate. By 1949 there were fourteen different parties represented in congress and a few more without representation. This atomization

---

6. For a discussion of these modifications see Mario Bernaschina González, *Constitución política y leyes complementarias* (Santiago: Editoria Jurídica de Chile, 1958), pp. 165ff.; and Heise, *op. cit.*, p. 97.

of political forces reflected a malfunction in the authoritistic mechanism.

The proliferation of political groups is symptomatic of the lack of a powerful cultural or political monistic center of attraction. It is the existence of such a void—at least in societies with authoritistic tendencies—that produces a rapid increase in the number and diversity of political groups. The relative degree of authoritistic malfunction is reflected in the popularity and strength of diverse political factions that potentially exist in every community.

The Radical governments, especially the two last ones, benefited from the restoration of authoritism accomplished under Arturo Alessandri's second term. Neither Ríos nor González Videla were able to contribute a charismatic element to the allegiance rendered to the system. On the contrary, their inability to perform the function of moderator by elevating themselves above everyday partisan politics tended to undermine the basis of the system. To operate within an authoritistic framework, the president has to be seen as a national leader who rules the country in pursuit of abstract ideas. Only under these circumstances can his rule be seen as just and worthy of allegiance by most citizens. The quasi-magical faculties expected of a *true* president could not be found in someone who behaved as a precinct politician. The frustration felt by the Chileans who saw presidents they thought unworthy of the office, led, in 1952, to the election of a man who claimed to be above politics.

In Search of a Caudillo

The election of ex-dictator Carlos Ibáñez to the presidency presents an insurmountable obstacle to those who try to explain the political development of Chile in terms of parties. Apparently Chile had a well established party system that had operated without interruption since 1932. These parties ran candidates for president and elected the congressmen. They appear to have been, therefore, experienced and well equipped for electoral battles. Furthermore, they had enough time to educate the electorate in the virtues of party politics, and the specific ideas and programs each of them supported. In spite of this apparent strength, a candidate who placed himself above partisan politics could be elected with support that cut across party lines.

Ibáñez' election must be ascribed primarily to his caudillistic appeal. The strong character and personality of Ibáñez fitted the public image of an effective national leader. His claim to be above party politics reinforced the belief that he could exercise national leadership and act as a moderating force among competing interests. Under the Radicals, Chile had been forced into a certain degree of political pluralization that in accordance with the nation's traditional characteristics was quickly developing into anarchy. The election of Ibáñez was a reaction to this situation—an attempt to bring about the kind of leadership the country could respond to and work under. Unfortunately, however, Ibáñez' rule did not differ as much from that of the Radicals as had been hoped by those who elected him.[7]

The continuing poliferation of political parties

7. Federico G. Gil., *The Political System of Chile* (Boston: Houghton Mifflin Co., 1966), touches upon the real reason for Ibáñez' election when he states: "If in 1952 these voters tried to escape their responsibilities by electing a father-figure who would take upon himself all their worries, they were soon disappointed. . . ." Indeed they were searching for a father figure— at least, that is the only explanation that is logically acceptable and historically consistent.

pointed to further political disintegration. Out of a total of thirty-six duly registered parties, twenty secured congressional representation by 1953 and sixteen did not. The number of parties was reduced by the 1957 congressional elections, but the general state of affairs remained basically unaltered. President Ibáñez legalized the Communist party, and under his administration the Popular Action Front (FRAP), composed of Socialists and Communists was formed. In 1957 the *Falange Nacional* changed its name to Christian Democratic Party.

Ibáñez' failure to develop effective caudillistic rule left the situation very much where he found it. The need for strong leadership that would rescue the country from bitter partisan politics and almost uninterrupted social and economic crisis was strongly felt. Therefore, when Jorge Alessandri, the son of Arturo, and a man of stern character, took it upon himself to run for president, he immediately became one of the favorite candidates. His strength was based upon his aloofness and desire to be above party politics. His personality was in conformity to caudillistic requirements. His major opponent was Salvador Allende, the candidate of the FRAP. Allende's strength was founded on his call for social reform.

Alessandri's caudillistic appeal won over Allende's call for a highly romanticized interpretation of political rationality. Once more the Chileans preferred a strong personal image over political rationalizations. The impact of the personal appeal was strong enough to overcome some other culturally familiar elements implied in Allende's program—idealism and organizational monism.

Jorge Alessandri's six years in power helped to solidify the system of presidential authoritism. The president carefully disassociated himself from partisan conflicts. He played the moderating role well with the consequence that the mistakes of his government were blamed on his ministers and not on him. Jorge Alessandri's rule revitalized the office he occupied. His degree of success can be measured by the fact that he appeared to have been more popular when he left than when he took office. Such popularity was attained in spite of his government's inability to deal effectively with the most pressing economic and social problems. His grip on the nation was such that during his term there was talk of changing the constitution to permit him to be reelected. The president's accomplishment in eliciting loyalty to his person and allegiance to the system he represented were not the result of specific accomplishments of his administration, but of his caudillistic personality.[8]

Christian Democracy and Frei

The elections of 1964 appear to corroborate the Chileans' proposed tendency toward authoritism and their predilection for caudillistic types. Eduardo Frei, the candidate of the Christian Democratic party, was elected by a wide margin over his two opponents—Salvador Allende and Julio Durán.[9] Frei's victory was sweeping and there

8. Lawrence Littwin, "An Integrated View of Chilean Foreign Policy," New York University, unpublished Ph.D. dissertation, 1967. In this study of the decision by the Chilean government to break relations with Cuba, the author deals in some detail with the operational characteristics of Alessandri s caudillistic rule.

9. The failure of Julio Durán, as a presidential candidate, was closely related to his non-caudillistic political personality. Durán was not able to disassociate himself, in the public mind, from intra-party strife and ward politics. The Chilean public appear to have thought of him as a slippery politician who was overreaching himself. There is little question that other factors came also to undermine Durán's candidacy. The inability of the Conservative, Liberal, and Radical parties to work together contrib-

is no doubt his appeal cut accross party lines.[10] It must be kept in mind, however, that a comparison between this and the preceding presidential election of 1958 would show that the new Christian Democratic votes came from the Conservative and Liberal parties.[11] Allende's strength in 1958 had been his appeal to rational romanticism and socialist militancy. In 1964, Frei, also the advocate of social and economic reforms, was able to undermine Allende's potential appeal. The Christian Democratic candidate combined the force of his caudillistic personality with the romantic concept of radical change within a system of law and order. Such a combination had the added advantage of preying on the fears aroused by Castro in Cuba.

The victory of Frei has been commonly explained in terms of his party's ideology and platform.[12] Such an explanation implies a high degree of rational behavior on the part of the voters, and it is usually more representative of the analyst's intellectual preconceptions and political orientation than of reality. An electorate that had chosen Carlos Ibáñez and Jorge Alessandri on the basis of their caudillistic personalities could not have been changed in so short a period of time. It is true that the Christian Democratic party had been gaining strength steadily since it changed its name in 1957, but its rapid

---

uted a great deal to his downfall. But in spite of any circumstantial reasons, Durán himself was his own worst enemy.

10. For a brief analysis of the election see Halperin, *op. cit.,* pp. 218ff. For a more detailed analysis see Federico G. Gil, *op. cit.,* and Charles J. Parrish, *The Chilean Presidential Election of September 4, 1964. Part I: An Analysis* (Washington, D.C.: Institute for the Comparative Study of Political Systems, 1965).

11. In 1964 the Socialist and Communist parties obtained a gain of 10% over their 1958 voting strength. See Appendix I.

12. For an example of this see Gil., *op. cit.,* pp. 306f.

advance was more the result of the caudillistic image of its leader than of the objective value of its philosophy.

The caudillistic appeal of Frei has also been made clear by the results of the congressional election of March 1965. Under the slogan "A Congress for Frei," the Christian Democrats achieved a sweeping victory. Out of a total of 147 seats in the House of Deputies and 21 in the Senate, the Christian Democrats elected 82 deputies and 12 senators. They obtained 41.1 per cent of the total vote.[13] This was an impressive victory for the party, but it was not a victory of the party. Such an overwhelming showing in congressional elections in the aftermath of a presidential contest won by a caudillistic leader was not new to Chile. In 1932 Arturo Alessandri's supporters won over 40 per cent of the votes in that year's congressional election; and in 1953, under the slogan "A Congress for Ibáñez," the congressional election resulted in an even greater victory for the supporters of the ex-dictator.[14] In those two instances, as well as in 1965, the electorate was reaffirming its confidence in the newly elected *caudillo*. To ascribe the victory of 1965 to any quick conversion of the Chilean people to the Christian Democratic faith would be, historically and politically, an expression of profound naiveté.

During his years in power Frei has been confronted with a dilemma. He can either accept institutional limitations to his executive power that tend to erode his caudillistic position—and authority and power—or he can enforce his will over prescribed regulations. The second

13. Charles J. Parrish, Arpad J. von Lazar and Jorge Tapia Videla, *The Chilean Congressional Election of March 7, 1965: An Analysis* (Washington, D.C.: Institute for the Comparative Study of Political Systems, 1967).

14. See Appendix II.

alternative would make him conform openly with the caudillistic principles of government. So far his position has been one of conforming to the existing constitutional and procedural order. On some occasions he appeared to have been tempted to overrule or bypass congress by going directly to the people in a caudillistic fashion, but in fact has not done so. More typical of his position was his acceptance of the congressional action of January 1967 that forbade him to leave the country after a state visit to the United States had been planned and announced.[15]

The unwillingness or inability of Frei to develop his caudillistic potential more fully cannot but weaken his political position. Whether his behavior reflects personally held beliefs, or the pressure of political groups supporting his regime,[16] the result is likely to be the same. To the degree that Frei is reluctant to use his caudillistic qualities, his ability to cary through his program of government will suffer. His ambivalent caudillistic performance has resulted, among other things, in internal strife within the Christian Democratic party and in a loosening of his hold over the electorate. In the municipal elections of 1967 the Christian Democratic party obtained 35.6 per

---

15. *New York Times,* January 18, 1967, 1:6.
16. Frei's support has come primarily from the conservative classes. If recent Chilean electoral statistics were analyzed, it would be easy to see that Christian Democratic strength has developed at the expense of the Conservative and Liberal parties. Both parties have lost electoral force in direct relation to Christian Democratic gains. The Radical party has also lost electoral strength in recent years, but in its case it cannot be readily assumed that its loss has been the Christian Democrat's gain. Given the socioeconomic composition, traditional anti-clericalism and past history of the Radical party, it would be more logical to look upon the Communists and Socialists as the probable beneficiaries. It could also be added that the corporate philosophical underpinnings of Christian Democracy are more palatable to Conservatives and Liberals than to Radicals.

cent of the vote—a decline of 5.5 per cent from the 1965 congressional election; and in the 1969 congressional elections the party suffered an even greater setback. In this last election, the Christian Democratic candidates obtained approximately 30 per cent of the vote.[17] This figure compares unfavorably with the party's presidential vote of 1967, and even more unfavorably with the 41.1 per cent the Christian Democrats secured in the preceding congressional elections of 1965.[18] After some years in power, and after having shown some reluctance to implement personal authoritism, or caudillistic rule, Frei's magic touch seems to be somewhat tarnished. The miracles have not been forthcoming, and his failure to live up to popular expectation seems to have taken its toll.

To believe that Christian Democracy, or any other philosophy of government, can alter the reality of Chile's political patterns is to underestimate the nature of the monistic and absolutistic inclinations latent in that country. Political parties and governmental ideologies have come and gone in Chile since the Spaniards arrived.[19] Without making assertions as to the nature of these tendencies that cannot be supported by evidence, it would only be logical to suppose they are still in operation. The political life of the country clearly points toward it.

17. *New York Times,* March 4, 1969, 8:1. The reference made in this report to the role played by Jorge Alessandri in the congressional elections is most interesting. It seems to support the caudillistic interpretation of his political appeal put forward in this book.

18. See Appendix II.

19. For a historical study of Chilean political parties see Alberto Edwards and Eduardo Frei, *Historia de los partidos políticos chilenos* (Santiago: Editorial del Pacífico, 1949); and Edmundo Montecinos Rozas, *Apuntaciones para el estudio de la evolución de los partidos políticos chilenos y de su proyección jurídica* (Santiago: Imprenta Dirección General de Prisiones, 1942).

The ability of President Frei to reform vital aspects of the country's economic and social order rests upon how well he adjusts his actions to the authoritistic configuration of the system he is operating in. Attempts to pluralize the governmental structure will only weaken it, thus forfeiting the opportunity for effective government. Frei's major handicap may be his ability to assimilate his own propaganda. Should he let his intellectual inclination for pluralism interfere with his nation's proclivity toward absolutistic monism, he will end his term as an ineffective president, and his party will lose electoral vitality, unless of course, a new *caudillo* takes over the helm.

VIII.

Conclusions

Through analysis of the Spanish colonial system and the political development of Chile, a theory of authoritism has been developed. This theory postulates that there is a basic organizational pattern in Chilean politics. From the days of the conquest, legitimate, absolutistic, and monistic rule appears to have been the form of government to which the inhabitants of the country most readily acquiesced. Furthermore, authoritistic rule seems to have been more conducive to stable government and socio-economic progress than the alternatives with which the country experimented. It has also been assumed that authoritistic government is in conformity with cultural and psychological forces deeply felt in the Chilean community, and had this not been the case, authoritism could never have flourished.

The phenomenon of authoritism has been stated but not investigated in detail. The purpose of this book has been to call attention to its existence rather than to analyze fully its internal complexity. The psychological, cultural, and sociological causes of authoritism have not been explored. Such an exploration is necessary if the phenomenon is to be understood in its proper perspective. The educational system, family structure, religious ideas, symbolic conceptions, leadership development, and patterns of group dynamics are but a few of the many aspects of collective life that are related to authoritism. But such a comprehensive analysis cannot be undertaken at present. The available information concerning Chilean life is not sufficient. More detailed knowledge of psychological trends and sociological characteristics woud be required. Therefore, this book has tried to develop a theoretical model that would make possible the discovery of the authoritistic phenomenon without trying to prod into the exact nature of the phenomenon itself.

The adjectives traditionally used to refer to Chilean regimes—autocratic, democratic, authoritarian, dictatorial, etc.—have failed to convey a clear picture of reality. The use of these adjectives has responded to a desire to judge and evaluate the political performance of the country according to ideas and institutions either developed in different lands under dissimilar circumstances, or created out of unrealistic conceptualizations. Such classifications have never corresponded to an analysis of the country's political reality. The cultural and psychological factors affecting conduct have never been taken into consideration for development of frames of reference that could explain Chilean political behavior. The rule of one man has always been called autocratic, dictatorial, or authoritarian, with no attention paid to the Chilean attitude toward such rule—to their willingness or lack of willingness to accept it and work under it. The violation of legal prescriptions has been judged with no understanding of the legitimizing factors that on many occasions rendered such violations legitimate and, therefore, legal in a more profound and meaningful sense. The votes obtained by political parties have been credited to their ideologies and platforms, leaving us at a loss to explain how parties that showed strength in municipal and congressional elections failed miserably in presidential contests. Accepted principles of psychological knowledge have been thrown out the window, and rationalizations have been taken as the motivating forces of behavior.[1]

The main concern of this book is to demonstrate that a phenomenon in existence for quite a few hundred years has been hidden by an unsystematic and deceptive phraseology. Whether the term authoritism is an adequate one or not is not the relevant point. The important issue is the pressing need to dispose of many prejudices and misconceptions if an understanding of Chilean and, more generally, Latin American political behavior and processes is to be gained.

In analyzing Chile—and the same case could be made for the rest of Latin America—systems of government have been classified according to their apparent structure rather than according to their functional or political cultural characteristics. The holding of elections has been seen as a democratic function without considering the actual meaning of such a process for those participating in it. Monistic rule has been branded as undemocratic without any attempt to evaluate the actual degree of participation and representation such rule provides. Economic factors have been linked to political developments

---

1. For examples on this type of analysis see Russell Fitzgibbon, "Pathology of Democracy in Latin America: A Political Scientist's Point of View," *The American Political Science Review,* XLIV, No. 1 (March 1950), p. 124; and James L. Busey, *Latin America: Political Institutions and Processes* (New York: Random House, 1964), p. 161.

without anyone bothering to explain how such relationships operate. The final test of any sound analysis is whether it enhances the ability to predict or not. Traditional interpretations of Chilean politics have failed that test. And it is in this respect that the validity of the authoritistic theory ought to be judged. The authoritistic interpretation of Chilean politics allows us to hypothesize about the political future of the country.

Political pluralism has traditionally failed in Chile. The relative high degree of stability the country has enjoyed has been the product of its adherence to a monistic system capable of eliciting the allegiance of the politically important sectors. It would be proper to predict that such a situation will not be altered in the near future. Leadership, to be successful, will have to remain caudillistic, or it will have to be firmly institutionalized. In either case, the president will be looked upon by most Chileans as the undisputed ruler of the nation, the leader who is to lead it in the name of an abstract concept of justice that takes precedence over written laws. Sharing of power will be seen as a sign of weakness, and it will lead to lack of confidence and support. The viable alternatives to authoritism, within the Chilean cultural context, are dictatorship and anarchy.

Chile, as a society, lacks sufficient social cohesiveness to permit the government to cease acting as a powerful collective unifying factor. If authoritism is destroyed, dictatorship will have to take its place, or the country will be plunged into chaos. The army will abstain from politics only as long as there is a civilian president who conforms to either the caudillistic or the institutional form of authoritism. Christian Democracy will last as a powerful political force in direct relation to its ability to work within the monistic-authoritistic pattern. The more *caudillos* the party places in the executive mansion, the longer it will be able to hold power. By the same token, Radicals, Socialists, and Communists will be only as successful as their ability to provide caudillistic figure allows them.

Perhaps the most immediate contribution the theory of authoritism has to offer is its concomitant interpretation of political participation. If democracy is defined in terms of a universally valid series of symbolic rituals, authoritism would not fall within its scope. But if democracy is understood in terms of political participation, it would have to be concluded that authoritism is conducive to it. A political system culturally accepted and understood, provides, by definition, more opportunities for participation than one that is not. In the former the people understand the mechanisms through which their opinions can be expressed and their interests defended. That such mechanisms are under the control of the executive cannot be taken, by itself, as a sign of ineffectiveness. On the other hand, a system of rules that is basically alien to the people of the country canot afford them a good opportunity for making their presence felt. If the preconception that there are only certain ways of providing for respresentation and participation is put aside, the representative and integrative qualities of authoritism might be better realized.[2]

Lastly, the authoritistic interpretation should provide analytical devices applicable not only to Chile but to the

2. Carl J. Friedrich, *Man and his Government* (New York: McGraw Hill Book Co., Inc., 1963), p. 100, points out that a classification of democracy "may refer simply to the actually existing order *as it is.*" (Author's italics). For an enlightened discussion of the different possible interpretations of democracy see G. E. G. Catlin, *Systematic Politics: Elementa Politica et Sociologica* (Toronto: University of Toronto Press, 1962), pp. 158ff.

rest of Latin America as well. The colonial origins of authoritism indicate that the system was introduced in all the Spanish colonies with similar degrees of success. The study of Chile should thus be of help in developing more acute comparative tools for the evaluation of the Latin American political systems. The importance of the study of Chile for a better understanding of Latin American political institutions and behavior is difficult to over-emphasize. It should be within this broader framework that the interpretations of authoritism, caudillism, and dictatorship offered in this work prove their final value.

Personal Leadership

In the interpretation of Chilean politics put forward in this book, charismatic leadership has been treated as providing grounds for legitimizing political rule, and, as such, it has been equated with personal authoritism. I would be less than honest if I did not acknowledge doubts surrounding the nature and quality of charisma. In recent years the concept of charisma has come under close scrutiny. The legitimizing quality of charisma has not been challenged, but there seem to be good reasons for limiting the scope of the term.[3] While realizing the dangers of employing the term in a misleading manner, I decided to retain it. The term "charisma" implies clear reference to some of the qualities that were to be emphasized in this study. Furthermore, any attempt to clarify the nature and scope of charismatic leadership would have taken the book afar from its objective.

I must admit, though, when referring to charisma I have meant a conception of personal leadership that tran-

---

3. For a discussion of legitimization see Claude Ake, *A Theory of Political Integration* (Homewood, Illinois: The Dorsey Press, 1967), pp. 51ff.

scends the boundaries of Weber's definition. As a legitimizing agent and social-political phenomenon, what I have described as personal authoritism comes very close to David Easton's definition of personal legitimacy.[4] The personal worth attached to the leaders, rather than their official positions or ideological commitments, is what gives them their legitimizing character. Such a relationship between the leader and the led, therefore, must be understood in psychological—not moral—terms.[5]

It should also be mentioned that the development of only two types of authoritism—personal and institutional—presents an implicit challenge to Max Weber's typology of legitimate authority. In the political history of Chile only institutional (traditional) and personal (charismatic) grounds for legitimacy appear. No instance of legitimization on rational grounds is found. This is no accident. Weber's rational grounds fall in the category of rationalization. Traditional and charismatic grounds are reflections of a clear emotional commitment to an institution or person; rational grounds rest "on a belief in the 'legality' of patterns of normative rules and the right of those elevated to authority under such rules to issue commands."[6] Weber further explains this "legal authority" as extending "to the persons exercising the authority of office under it only by virtue of the formal legality of their commands and only within the scope of authority of the office."[7] Such a cenception ignores the high degree of emotional attachment the acceptance of authority implies.

4. *A Systems Analysis of Political Life* (New York: John Wiley & Sons, Inc., 1965), pp. 302ff.
5. David Easton, *The Political System: An Inquiry into the State of Political Science* (New York: Alfred H. Knopf, 1964), p. 132.
6. Weber, *op. cit.*, p. 328.
7. *Ibid.*

The legitimizing process is firmly grounded in a psychological reaction of a very basic character. Rational legitimization, on the other hand, is explained by Weber as resulting from a conscious process. Through this process, authority is accepted as legitimate. Such a process of legitimization would differ in kind from the emotion-bound traditional and charismatic instances. It is my contention that legitimacy can only be secured through the emotional commitment suggested in tradition and charisma, and cannot be primarily the result of a conscious process of acceptance. The phenomenon Weber describes as "rational" is, at best, a rationalization for a system that is accepted on more profound psychological bases, or, at worst, an attempt to see legitimacy where it does not exist.

Authoritism and Latin America

The analysis of Chilean politics presented in this book should provide some guidelines for the study of other Latin American countries.[8] The same authoritistic elements encountered in colonial Spanish America seem to have been present in the Portuguese and French colonial systems. The tendency toward legitimization through personal leadership is present throughout the area. Important differences do exist between the political institutions and processes operating in various countries in the area, but enough cultural variables are shared by them to allow for considerable similarities.

The political patterns present in these countries have enough resemblance to one another to make references to "Latin American political behavior" frequent. Lack of

8. Spain and Portugal should be included in this category. What is said here about Latin America is equally applicable to them.

stability, tendency toward one-man rule, proliferation of constitutions, involvement of the military in the running of the government, and ineffectiveness of legislatures and judiciaries, have all been among the political traits exhibited by the Latin American nations. Such affinities have prevailed in spite of variations in ethnic composition and geographic location and structure.

There are many disparities among the countries that form Latin America. These distinctions are clearly visible in many aspects of their social and economic lives. Even political style sometimes appears to change from country to country. Notwithstanding apparent or real variations, some psychological and cultural patterns seem to be germane to the whole area. The republican, as well as colonial, history of the region testifies to this effect.

It should be possible to construct behavioral theories for the area as a whole. These hypotheses would have to be based on cultural characteristics present in the countries, or communities, under study. These cultural factors would constitute constant elements for theoretical speculation. Once formulated, the hypotheses should prove useful in uncovering areas of similarities and disparities. The testing of the hypotheses, whenever possible, would help in ascertaining the existence or lack of existence of common patterns of political behavior among the countries of Latin America.

Some of the prevailing political characteristics could be explained in terms of the common, or quite similar, colonial background and the influence this background has retained. If this is done, and this is what has been done in analyzing authoritism, it would be necessary to remember that the so-called cultural influence is but a fictitious etiological theoretical device.[9] That is, it is as-

---

9. For a similar interpretation of culture see A. Irving Hallowell,

sumed that the given way of doing something responds to a series of factors unknown to us: the character of human nature, the forces present in the determination of collective behavior, the psychological function of leadership, etc. Therefore, the abstraction "cultural influence" is employed to signify the result of undetermined elements.[10]

A political phenomenon explained on the basis of the cultural forces motivating it is often the same as stating that an explanation for it is not available. The individual and collective mechanisms provoking the political action are not understood in their proper perspective. This is not to say that such a phenomenon cannot be observed, or even predicted, but simply that by using the cultural abstraction we are confessing our ignorance of its causes.

The interpretation of authoritism clearly falls within the realm of abstractions, but because it is abstract does not mean it is useless. Science is full of examples of knowledge attained through the correlation of factors whose individual origins have remained unknown. It is thus feasible to proceed cautiously in the unearthing of the political expressions of Latin American culture and to make predictions on the basis of such discoveries. But it would be completely out of order to confuse cultural expressions with the motivating forces of behavior. That a relationship between them must exist is obvious. To take the former for the latter would only lead astray.[11]

Culture and Experience (New York: Schocken Books, 1967), pp. 33ff.

10. For a contemporary analysis of different conceptions of culture see Bidney, *op. cit.,* pp. 23ff.

11. On the relationship of culture and behavior see Bernard Berelson and Gary A. Steiner, *Human Behavior* (New York: Harcourt, Brace & World, Inc., 1964). On the influence of culture upon personality see Anthony F. C. Wallace, *Culture and Personality* (New York: Random House, 1961).

Aware of the proper scope of cultural explanations, it can be asserted that traditional Iberian patterns of political behavior are present in Latin American societies. The vitality of such traits has been preserved by a forceful system of cultural discrimination. Negroes and Indians have been precluded from bringing alien elements into their societies to such an extent that the political ways of the whites have not suffered any major change. Indians and Negroes have been integrated into Latin American societies only after they have learned how to function within the established Iberian cultural heritage. Nonintegrated individuals and groups have been kept at the margin of society and political participation. Negroes and Indians, as individuals, have successfully taken part in the political affairs of their countries in many instances, but as representatives of potentially different political institutions and concepts their contribution has been nil.[12]

Due to the apparent similarities in the political systems of the area, it can be argued that the study of Chilean political practices has a validity that transcends the boundaries of that country. The relatively higher degree of political stablity achieved by Chile since independence has been commonly used as a sign of the existence of profound differences between her and the rest of the countries in the area. Through the authoritistic interpretation of Chilean political stability the opposite point can now be stated. The development of a fairly stable system of government in Chile has not been the result of the country's

12. For a most interesting discussion of Latin American attitudes toward Spain and themselves see Leopoldo Zea, *The Latin-American Mind* (Norman, Oklahoma: University of Oklahoma Press, 1963), pp. 3ff. Disregard for Indian and Negro cultural values can be seen in a work as recent as German Arciniegas' *Latin America: A Cultural History* (New York: Alfred A. Knopf, 1967).

uniqueness, but of its ability to accommodate structurally political forces common to the whole region.

Chile's ability to rebuild authoritism within a republican frame is what sets her apart from most of her sister republics. It must be added that Chile is not alone in this achievement. Mexico since the revolution is another case of successful authoritistic development under republican forms. Potentially, all Latin American countries are prone to follow the authoritistic path if the opportunity arises. Perón in Argentina, Vargas in Brazil, and Gómez in Venezuela are just three contemporary cases illustrating this point. Why only Chile and Mexico have been able to fulfill the potential for any continuous period of time in an institutionalized form, is not easy to determine. Speculation focuses on historical and ecological factors. Assuming that cultural elements remained constant through the area, the logical conclusion would be to search for either environmental forces, or idiosyncratic historical circumstances as responsible for the creation of authoritistic rule in only these two countries.

It could be argued that ecological factors would tend to influence cultural ones and, therefore, that the differences between Chile and Mexico, and the rest of Latin America, are substantive rather than formal. This line of thought has some theoretical validity and cannot be completely discarded, but it cannot be accepted as a working hypothesis unless some evidence in its behalf is brought forward. It would be necessary to demonstrate how environmental forces affected meaningful changes in the prevailing cultural predispositions. Then it would be simpler to assume that the same cultural elements when combined with different historical or ecological circumstances produce different results.

The parallels between Mexico and Chile should interest students of comparative politics. After the revolutionary chaos and the shaky government of Venustiano Carranza, Mexico fell into the hands of Alvaro Obregón. The new leader was able to consolidate military and civilian control in his hands. His caudillistic personality elicited allegiance, and his political instincts led to the elimination of competing potential *caudillos* and enemies.

Obregón's rule was basically caudillistic and, therefore, of limited stability. As with Portales in Chile, his assassination paved the way for the depersonalization of presidential control. His successor, Plutarco Elías Calles, was also very much of a *caudillo*. Although he stepped down from the presidency in 1928, at the end of his legal term, the three succeeding presidents had no control over the country and were at his mercy. Calles' decision to preserve the constitutional façade may have contributed to the institutionalization of executive supremacy.

The next president was Lázaro Cárdenas, who quickly turned to the task of eliminating Calles' political influence. Cárdenas himself had the qualities of a *caudillo,* and during his term authoritism became properly institutionalized. His power was final and absolute, and as such it matched the nation's expectancy of what presidential power should be. At the same time, executive prerogatives were to be used for the benefit of the country and were carried out in the name of justice. The presidency began to function as a moderating power.

Since 1934 Mexico has adhered to a monistic system of government in which the president is ascribed final control. The chief executive runs the country with the acquiescence of all other political officials. As the last effective tribunal of appeals, the president's decision is final, and his power is increased by his ability to choose his successor. This organization of power has been consolidated through the *Partido Revolucionario Institucional,* or P.R.I. This semi-official organization provides the effective machinery through which presidential supremacy is implemented. The development of a system of institutional authoritism appears largely responsible for the political stability the country has achieved. Such stable government has, in turn, contributed greatly to the country's recent economic and social progress.[13]

The case of Mexico validates some of the assumptions made concerning Chile. The authoritistic experiment seems to have provided a set of rules that are accepted and understood by the inhabitants of the country. Presidential supremacy encountered no real opposition so long as the caudillistic role of the president was clear. The political disturbances that have taken place in Mexico recently, as well as the apparent increase in public discontent with the existing system, are probably connected with the non-caudillistic personalities of the country's last three presidents. Adolfo Ruíz Cortines (1952-1958), Adolfo López Mateos (1958-1964) and Gustavo Díaz Ordáz (1964-) became presidents not on the basis of their public appeal, but through the party machinery. In the public eye they have been more successful politicians than popular leaders. Their personal appeal is a far cry from that exercised by the revolutionary presidents who built the system. Obregón, Calles, and Cárdenas strengthened the presidency by means of their powerful personalities and caudillistic image, but the more recent executives have relied on the office for power and prestige. Recent

---

13. For an analysis of post-revolutionary Mexico see Frank R. Brandenburg, *The Making of Modern Mexico* (Englewood Cliffs, New Jersey: Prentice-Hall, Inc., 1964). For a study of Mexican political institutions see L. Vincent Padgett, *The Mexican Political System* (Boston: Houghton Mifflin Company, 1966).

developments in Mexico seem to indicate that there may be a limit to the ability of the office to support weak leaders. But whether the system is now deteriorating through lack of caudillistic personalities or not, it has provided for more participation in politics than its predecessors, and it seems to have been conducive to a higher degree of social and economic improvement than that existing before it.

Stability and Political Originality

In a way, Mexico and Chile have shown more political originality than the other Latin American countries. Their authoritistic creations have given them the internal security, psychological as well as political, necessary for experimentation. By being less concerned with imitating foreign formulas of political organization, they have been able to develop a more pragmatic attitude toward political institutions. This interrelation between authoritism and political originality may seem contradictory at first, but it is not.

Authoritism has meant for Chile and Mexico the citizens' recognition of their own cultural inclinations. The creation of such a system required them to cease trying to adjust their political lives to principles and institutions originated in England, France, or the United States. Only through a greater readiness to face and deal with their own cultural realities were these two countries in a position to experiment with authoritism. There is no assumption that such a process was a totally conscious one. But whether conscious or subconscious, it was an act of political creativity unmatched by the rest of Latin America, most of whose nations stubbornly insist on organizational forms of alien origin.

The success of authoritism in Mexico and Chile has been in marked contrast to the endemic lack of stability characteristic of almost all other Latin American nations. Their propensity to chaos and disorder stems from systems of government lacking the necessary cultural bases upon which they could operate. In short, their governments do not function because they cannot function. This seems to be a tautology, but it is not. Pluralistic schemes have been forced on Latin America quite frequently. Initially, native intellectuals, anxious to imitate the European and American examples, introduced foreign models hoping they would act as magic balm for the political ills of their countries. These simplistic solutions (still very much in vogue) denoted an escapist tendency and a reluctance to engage in the objective study of the problems at hand. Such an approach also connoted the superficiality of Latin American political thought, and, perhaps, the colonizing vigor of Western European ideas and institutions.

Later, external forces joined in the attempt to make Latin American nations conform to political principles and institutions purported to have universal validity. The proponents of pluralistic schemes of government still go on explaining the continuous fiasco of their proposals in terms of temporary maladjustments that, once corrected, would remove all obstacles to the fulfillment of their goals. They are quite reluctant to admit, even hypothetically, that political pluralism, at least in its Anglo-Saxon variety, just does not work in Latin America. Their aversion is logically unexplainable. The advocates of political pluralism for the area comport themselves as propagandists of a system rather than as students of reality. Their position is far from liberal. They do not only refuse to accept Latin Americans for what they are, but insist on imposing upon them political systems that would, in all probability, retard or preclude social and economic change. In the name of democracy they contribute to chaos and dictatorship.

Chile, Uruguay, and Costa Rica are the countries commonly offered as examples of the viability of pluralism in Latin America. Chile has already been dealt with at some length; and if no other part of its analysis remains valid, it is hoped the failure of pluralistic attempts will. The history of Uruguay and Costa Rica provides no better grounds for expecting successful pluralistic political development. The recent return of Uruguay to a presidential system is one of the many instances that corroborate their monistic orientation.

Today Costa Rica and Uruguay are used much in the same way as Argentina and Colombia were used before them—as living examples of political pluralism.[14] At present it is accepted that such references to Argentina and Colombia were premature, but the acknowledgement of the error has not led to a more skeptical opinion concerning Uruguay and Costa Rica. A few years of apparent legal continuity and absence of revolts are accepted as final outcomes without any analysis of the nature of such continuity or the role of the military. Any skeptical observer—and all serious observers should be skeptical—would tend to doubt the validity of shortlived trends. This skepticism would grow if the explanations for such

14. For such interpretations concerning Uruguay see Milton J. Vanger, "Uruguay Introduces Government by Committee," *The American Political Science Review,* (June 1954), pp. 501ff.; and Russell Fitzgibbon, "Argentina and Uruguay: A Tale of Two Attitudes," *Pacific Spectator,* (Winter 1954) . For a similar interpretation concerning Costa Rica see James L. Busey, "Foundations of Political Contrast: Costa Rica and Nicaragua," *The Western Political Quarterly,* (September 1958).

trends fail to take into account the past of the countries and the character of their political culture.

Uruguay and Costa Rica may prove to be, in the long run, departures from the rule. In the meantime, however, there is little evidence to assume this is the case.[15] Both countries have conformed for many years to the political modes characteristic of the area. Therefore, in determining the nature and functional character of their present systems, an analysis of their authoritistic inclinations should be of assistance. Perhaps such a study also should be extended to Venezuela since this country has lately been added to the Chile, Uruguay, and Costa Rica list as an example of "democratic" behavior.

Cuba is another country to which the application of the authoritistic hypothesis could produce unexpected results. A great deal could be learned about the country's political past and present regime if it is assumed that its culture contains authoritistic elements. One of the first conclusions would be that Fidel Castro conforms to the *caudillo* role and that, therefore, his ability to secure allegiance to his person constitutes the legitimizing force of his system. It could also be maintained that communism is but a rationalization for Castro's rule. That thousands of Cubans who did not consider themselves communists one day, were willing to convert the next, provides a clue as to Castro's ability to elicit allegiance, as well as to the superficial roots of communism in Cuba. It is most likely that most of the followers of Castro became communists because he asked them to. Their communism did not spring from intellectual conviction or

---

15. Michael Weinstein (in an unpublished manuscript titled "A Critique of Democracy in Uruguay and Costa Rica") sees little reason to assume the development of pluralistic trends in those countries.

educational training, but from an emotional desire to identify with their leader.[16]

Contemporary analyses of Cuba have tried to explain the events taking place in that island using various hypotheses, all of which have in common elements of economic determinism.[17] Notwithstanding the importance of economic issues, explaining Castro's success in those terms is highly misleading. It would miss the basis for Castro's present role: the proclivity in Cuban culture for a quasimagical, monistic, and absolutistic center of authority and power.[18] Such an orientation was not created by economic necessities, and Castro's hold will not be weakened through economic failures.

As long as Castro himself is in power, his regime will be only temporarily stable. Caudillism could be under certain circumstances conducive to institutionalized authoritism, but it could also preclude it. In Chile and Mexico, the disappearance of Portales and Obregón preceded the institutionalizing process. It is not difficult to see how the presence of the *caudillo* may create difficulties to the institutionalization of authority. His own personal attitude is not necessarily the determinant factor. In spite of the *caudillo's* wishes, the force of his image could be so strong as to block any transfer of allegiance from him to an institution. This appears to have been the case with

16. For an analysis of the development of charismatic rule in Cuba under Castro see Andrés Suárez, *Cuba: Castroism and Communism* (Cambridge, Massachusetts: The M.I.T. Press, 1967), pp. 78ff.

17. For an example of this kind of analysis see Boris Goldenberg, *The Cuban Revolution and Latin America* (New York: Frederick A. Praeger, Publishers, 1965).

18. A perceptive description of some of Cuba's cultural characteristics is provided in Wyatt MacGaffey and Clifford R. Barnett, *Twentieth-Century Cuba* (New Haven, Connecticut: HRAF Press, 1962).

Portales. He refused the vice-presidency and moved away from Santiago but the people of Chile kept looking upon him as the actual center of political power. This situation could easily repeat itself in Cuba if Fidel Castro tries to move into the background in an attempt to institutionalize the revolution. As long as he is alive and in Cuba, there is little chance of transferring allegiance away from him.

The study of contemporary political developments in Cuba is also interesting because of the way communist ideology has been used. Communist theories have been used in the same way as English, American, and French political thought are so commonly used in Latin America. The Latin American tendency to imitate rather than create seems to have found a new model. For the first time in the region, Russian institutions and Marxist thought have been applied in the hope they will alter reality. The script is new, but the act is old. This new attempt to force reality into ideal molds will probably not fare any better than its predecessors.

When Castro and his government are analyzed in the light of their caudillistic nature and tendency to copy foreign forms, the conclusions—startling to some, no doubt —that the Cuban leader and his system are culturally conservative must be reached.[19] In regard to the functional characteristics of the political system within which he operates, Fidel Castro has exhibited little imagination or desire for change. Perhaps Castro himself should not be made responsible for this state of affairs. He is, after all, faced with an irreconcilable dilemma. For to bring about the social and economic changes to which he is committed,

---

19. For a candid exposition of Castro's culture-bound views concerning sex, the family, and related matters see Lee Lockwood, *Castro's Cuba, Cuba's Fidel* (New York: The Macmillan Company, 1967).

he must make sure he has a firm hold on the political apparatus. The necessity to tightly control the government forces him to follow the most traditional and safest of all roads, caudillism. His desire to be an innovator in one area forces him to be a conservative in the other. Castro's dilemma is complicated by the fact that his cultural conservatism may cast a shadow, in the long run, over his social and economic goals. The longer he adheres to caudillistic rule the less the chances that his system will survive him.

The cases of Mexico, Costa Rica, Uruguay, and Cuba have been mentioned, in addition to Chile, as deserving special attention. They have been mentioned not because there is more validity to their study than other nations in the area, but because some points are easier to make with them.[20] Special attention should be given to each individual Latin American nation. Within the context of Latin American politics, the analysis of Chile presented in this book is only a first attempt to open new avenues of investigation and research. Needless to say, the assertions and conclusions that have been put forward, in spite of their affirmative tone, have only the tentative character proper to theoretical speculation. Such ideas have been submitted in the conviction that the creation of new hypotheses is an imminent necessity if the behavioral and functional qualities of Latin American politics are to be understood.

---

20. Venezuela, under its recently elected president, Rafael Caldera, provides a good subject for comparison. The christian democratic party—COPEI—allows us an opportunity to identify qualties which may belong to the christian democratic movement in Latin America in general, and qualities peculiar to the country in question. It would also be of great interest to compare the nature of Caldera s leadership to Frei's.

Appendix I

Chile—Recent Presidential Elections

			Backing
1938	Pedro Aguirre Cerda (2)	212,000	Radicals, Socialists, Communists (PF)
	Gustavo Ross	199,000	Conservatives, Liberals
1942	Juan Antonio Ríos (2)	260,034	Radicals, Socialists, Communists
	Carlos Ibáñez	204,635	Conservatives, Liberals, Nazis
1946	Gabriel González Videla	192,207	Radicals, Communists
	Eduardo Cruz Coke	142,441	Falange, Socialists, Christian Socialists
	Fernando Alessandri	131,023	Conservatives, Liberals
	Bernando Ibáñez	12,114	Socialists
1952	Carlos Ibáñez	46.8%	non-political
	Arturo Matte	27.8%	Conservatives, Liberals
	Pedro Alfonso	19.9%	Radicals
	Salvador Allende	5.5%	Socialists
1958	Jorge Alessandri	31.6%	United Conservatives, Liberals
	Salvador Allende	28.9%	Socialists, Communists (FRAP)
	Eduardo Frei	20.7%	Christian Democrats
	Luis Bossay	15.6%	Radicals
	Antonio Zamorano	3.3%	leftists (former FRAP member)
1964	Eduardo Frei (1)	56.1%	Christian Democrats, United Conservatives, Liberals
	Salvador Allende	38.9%	Socialists, Communists (FRAP)
	Julio Durán	5.0%	Radicals

NOTES: (1) Eduardo Frei was the only candidate automatically elected, having received 50% + of the total vote. The others were all chosen by the legislature.

(2) Only the major candidates are listed.

Appendix II

CHILE—Recent Congressional Elections

PARTIES		1925	1932	1937	1941	1945	1949	1953	1957	1961	1965
Conservative	(1)	19.8%	16.9%	21.3%	17.1%	23.6%	22.7%	10.1%	13.8%	14.3%	5.4%
Liberal		32.4	18.8	20.7	14.0	17.9	18.0	10.9	15.3	16.1	10.1
Radical		21.4	18.2	18.7	21.7	20.0	21.7	13.3	21.5	21.4	12.8
Christian Democratic	(2)	—	—	—	3.4	2.6	3.9	2.9	9.4	15.4	41.1
Socialist	(3)	—	5.7	11.2	16.7	12.8	9.3	14.1	10.7	10.8	10.5
Communist	(4)	—	—	4.2	11.8	10.3	—	—	—	11.4	11.2
Other	(5)	26.4	40.4	23.9	15.3	22.8	24.4	48.7	29.3	10.6	8.9
Total		100.0%	100.0%	100.0%	100.0%	100.0%	100.0%	100.0%	100.0%	100.0%	100.0%

NOTES: (1) The Conservative party changed its name in 1957 to the United Conservative party.

(2) This party was known until 1957 as the "Falange Nacional". That year it united with the break-off Christian Socialist wing of the Conservative party to form the Christian Democratic party.

(3) The percentages tabulated for the Socialists until 1957 belong to many varied and everchanging Socialist groups. In 1957 the last two Socialist groups merged to form the Socialist party.

(4) The Communist Party was outlawed from 1948 to 1958.

(5) "Other" includes: minor parties, temporary associations, null votes, blank votes. The disproportionately large amounts in 1932 and 1953 were due to associations favoring the programs of Arturo Alessandri and Carlos Ibáñez, respectively.

Appendix III

CHILE—Recent Municipal Elections

PARTIES	1944[1]	1947	1950	1956	1960	1963[3]	1967[4]
Conservative[5]	22%	21%	26%	18%	14%	11.4%	} 14.6[6]%
Liberal	14	14	16	12	16	13.2	
Radical	24	21	24	23	21	21.6	16.5
Falange[7]	3	4	4	7	14	22.0	35.6
Socialist[8]	7	8	10	11	9	11.5	14.2
Communist[2]	8	16	—	—	9	12.7	15.0
Total	78%	84%	80%	71%	83%	92.4%	95.9%

Notes: [1]The 1944 to 1960 figures are approximations from a graph in Gil's *The Political System of Chile.*

[2]The Communist party was outlawed from 1948 to 1958.

[3]Figures given by Gil in his *The Political System of Chile.*

[4]Figures are taken from *The New York Times* (usually incomplete).

[5]In 1957 the Conservative party changed its name to the United Conservative party.

[6]In 1967 the United Conservative party and liberal party ran together as the Nationalist party.

[7]In 1957 the Falange merged with the Christian Socialist wing of the Conservative party to form the Christian Democratic party.

[8]Up to 1957 there were various socialist groups all of which are included under the heading "Socialist." In 1957 the last two remaining groups merged to form the Socialist party.